LESSONS LEARNED:
THE KINDERGARTEN SURVIVAL GUIDE FOR PARENTS

✏️ The Kindergarten Survival Book ✏️

JEANNIE PODEST

To Nancy,
Enjoy your "Lessons"!
Love you "Broham"!
♡ Jeannie xo

BALBOA
PRESS
A DIVISION OF HAY HOUSE

Balboa Press books may be ordered through booksellers or by contacting:

Balboa Press
A Division of Hay House
1663 Liberty Drive
Bloomington, IN 47403
www.balboapress.com
1 (877) 407-4847

Because of the dynamic nature of the Internet, any web addresses or links contained in this book may have changed since publication and may no longer be valid. The views expressed in this work are solely those of the author and do not necessarily reflect the views of the publisher, and the publisher hereby disclaims any responsibility for them.

The author of this book does not dispense medical advice or prescribe the use of any technique as a form of treatment for physical, emotional, or medical problems without the advice of a physician, either directly or indirectly. The intent of the author is only to offer information of a general nature to help you in your quest for emotional and spiritual well-being. In the event you use any of the information in this book for yourself, which is your constitutional right, the author and the publisher assume no responsibility for your actions.

Any people depicted in stock imagery provided by Thinkstock are models, and such images are being used for illustrative purposes only. Certain stock imagery © Thinkstock.

Printed in the United States of America.

ISBN: 978-1-4525-9467-5 (sc)
ISBN: 978-1-4525-9469-9 (hc)
ISBN: 978-1-4525-9468-2 (e)

Library of Congress Control Number: 2014905204

Balboa Press rev. date: 03/31/2014

To moms and dads everywhere:
you are your child's first teachers. Thank you
for allowing me to share in your journey.

Childhood is a journey, not a race.—Author Unknown

Contents

Foreword

My youngest sister, Jeannie, had a calling to be a kindergarten teacher. Since her return to teaching after a break from raising her own children, she has been in the kindergarten classroom, and there has never been a better fit. The parents and the children respect and admire Jeannie so much; they love and *trust* her. She would often be the resource parents went to with questions regarding their child or a situation at school. Mostly, parents would look to her to calm their fears or answer their questions: Were their children reading at the proper level? Were their social skills where they should be? Should they have their children in more extracurricular activities, or will they be ready for first grade? Kindergarten has changed over the years to the point where parents are as worried about their child in kindergarten as they are in college. Jeannie's experience and demeanor bring a calmness to the parent community, and that needs to be shared more broadly. After years of working with students and parents, and realizing that every class brings new students but very similar fears and concerns from the parents, Jeannie has written this book. She has talked about this for many years, and we are so happy that she has delivered this information.

When I wrote the foreword, I was excited about the opportunity to talk about my sister. Jeannie is the teacher you will remember when you are fifty years old. She is the teacher parents secretly hope their child will have. She is the teacher many other teachers respect and admire. She is there for the children, and her love of the five year old audience is infectious.

I am extremely proud of Jeannie. She is a wonderful wife, mother, daughter, sister, and friend. But what is unique to Jeannie Podest is the responsibility she carries as a kindergarten teacher; it is sacred to her. She has always been outspoken on the unique needs of the child moving up from preschool into kindergarten. She has also been extremely consistent and productive in building the best learning environment for the child *and* parents. As a sister, I am proud. As a parent, I trust her implicitly. Listen to her, laugh with her, learn from her, and educate your child with her. You and your child will greatly benefit! Enjoy your lessons!

Kathleen Martorano

Preface

This book was written as a gift to parents whose children are starting kindergarten. My intention is to give you every insight I have as a mother and as a teacher. Whether this is your first child going into kindergarten, your only child, your last child, or you've had a gap in time where you haven't been in a kindergarten classroom for a while, this book is for you. I have always found it fascinating and incredible that the most important job in the world—being a parent—comes with absolutely no guidelines! No manual or how-to book. I know I could have used one back when I was starting out, so I felt the need to write one for you.

The idea for writing this book came to me when I would share stories from my class with family and friends. I always got the same response: "You should write a book." I thought about it for a long time. I had always considered myself a decent writer but had never written a book before—I didn't even know how to begin. I didn't know anyone in the publishing world, nor did I have a single connection. What I did have, though, was an open mind, strong will, and determination. I felt like I had a message to share and a story to tell and I just couldn't let it go. So I prayed for some sort of guidance to point me in the right direction. I started paying attention to the inside covers of books to see who published some of my favorite titles.

Two years prior, I had the pleasure and good fortune to meet and spend an afternoon in Tucson, Arizona, with world-renowned author and equine therapist Wyatt Webb. This experience changed my life—forever. I later purchased and devoured his books *It's Not about the Horse* and *What to Do When You Don't Know What to Do* and noticed they were published by Hay House Publishing. I had also been following and falling in love with a "wellness warrior" named Kris Carr. I purchased one of her books, *Crazy Sexy Diet*, highlighting and dog-earing each page the whole way through. I looked inside the cover … huh. Hay House Publishing. Not long after, I was reading one of my favorite children's books, *Incredible You!* by Dr. Wayne Dyer, to my class. I have read that book to my students for years and never once noticed who published that book. Hay House strikes again! Wow! This was incredible—I had never even heard of this company before and it kept coming up.

One day last spring I received a brochure in the mail for a Hay House writers' workshop that would take place in New York City that June. There would be four key speakers—Reid Tracy, CEO of Hay House Publishing; Nancy Levin, Hay House author; Gabrielle Bernstein, Hay House author and motivational speaker; and Hay House author and health crusader Kris Carr. *Kris Carr? I'm going!* I was thrilled at the thought of hearing her speak live. I had admired and respected her work and her dedication to healthy living, and now I was going to hear her in person. This for me was the thrill of a lifetime.

Well, the weekend finally came and off I went by myself for two days to take part in this workshop. The weekend and the workshop were a dream come true. I learned so much from all four of these people about writing, publishing, making the most of opportunities that present themselves, making things happen, and never giving up, and as Kris Carr said over and over that weekend—about keeping the faith. I have kept the faith and here I am. I've written my first book.

I could never have seen this project through if it wasn't for the inspiration of these four people and for all the people in the room that weekend. Their stories also inspired me and made me realize I wasn't alone in my fear. They were feeling it too. We had learned about traditional publishing versus self-publishing. Self-publishing was something I really didn't know too much about before the workshop, and it sounded like the way to go for me. I committed to working with Balboa Press, the self-publishing division of Hay House Publishing. As I was nearing the end of my first rough draft for this book, my fear was getting the better of me again. *What am I thinking? Who do I think I am writing a book? What if no one ever reads it?* I was getting the feeling that I had gotten myself in way over my head. But in true divine form, the good Lord sent me one final sign of encouragement.

My oldest son, a senior in high school, was having a motivational speaker come to his school to address the entire student body. My son came home from school that day and was very moved and affected by the speaker's lecture. Apparently this woman had such a compelling story to share that they were offering an evening presentation as well. I wanted to go hear her, but it was on a school night and a work night and it just never seems easy to get out of the house on those nights.

As I was tossing the idea around in my head, I started going through the mail. In front of me was a Hay House holiday pamphlet profiling certain books that would make special holiday gifts. I flipped it over, and who did I see a picture of but the speaker going to my son's school! The speaker was Immaculee Ilibagiza, and her story was her *New York Times* bestselling novel *Left to Tell* published by—you guessed it—Hay House Publishing. *Okay, God, I get it! I'll go and I will hear her speak.* A friend of mine said she was going to attend and had an extra ticket for me. (Thanks, Lisa!) Listening to Immaculee's heartbreaking story of losing her family during the Rwandan genocide in 1994 was only part of her message. She was also sharing her journey of writing and eventually publishing her book. How one day in New York City "happenstance" (a.k.a. divine intervention) took place, and she met world-famous writer Dr. Wayne Dyer. The rest of her story is history. Her courage inspired me to finish my book and share my insights.

I hope what you read and learn here helps you and your child to not only survive but to thrive in kindergarten! Life can be confusing and a little overwhelming at times—we need to help each other out when we can.

I hope this book helps you. I have been bestowed tremendous good fortune and countless blessings to do what I do for a living. Some people call teaching a job, a profession, or a vocation. I don't really call it anything because it's just what I do. Like breathing and blinking, it's second nature to me. I have never felt like it's something that takes time out of my life or keeps me away from doing what I really wanted to do. To see life through five and six year old eyes, every day, is something that has made my life richer. To smile and laugh each day is something I wish everyone could experience when they go to work. I take none of it for granted.

When I look back on how I got to be where I am in my life, it all adds up and makes perfect sense -although I didn't always understand where I was being led. God had a plan, and I'm glad I heard his call. I am so very grateful for each and every student I have taught thus far and for their families too. As you have learned from me, I have learned from you as well.

Although I share my experiences with you, I have changed the name of every person in this book to keep their experiences private. The stories and references are all true—the names are not.

Chapter 1

From the Cradle to Crayons

So you have a baby, and you are so busy loving and caring for this child that you don't even notice how quickly the first few years have passed you by. Of course everyone tells you this is going to happen, but it's one of those things you can't really understand until you go through it yourself. Infancy, toddlerhood, the preschool years, and before we know it—kindergarten! How on earth did that happen so fast? It's such a big step, and it's really the beginning of formal education as we know it. There are so many different things to think about and various decisions to make regarding the beginning of this journey.

Many people base their decision of where they are going to live or where to buy a house based on the public school system in a particular area. Others research different private schools. No matter what your intention or desire is, you are giving this next step a lot of consideration, as you should. Once you decide on the school, there is plenty for parents to think about. This book is here to guide you through this wonderful, exciting, and sometimes overwhelming journey.

I very clearly remember the first time someone mentioned to me that I had to register my son for school. It was only January, and he was still four years old. I panicked. *What? No one told me this before! Does everyone else know about this?* September seemed so far away. I remember wishing at that exact moment—and many times since—that I had some kind of handbook or guide to tell me what to do or what I needed to know. After all, I had lived by my *What to Expect When You're Expecting* book each time I was pregnant, rereading it each time as if I had never had a baby before. Yes, I had a wonderful mother and two older sisters to help me, but I wanted to curl up in bed at night when everything was finally quiet and just really take it all in. Correction—I wanted to *soak* it all in. I wanted to know everything I should know about my child starting kindergarten. So over the years I started making mental notes, which became scribbles on paper. The scribbles became pages, and the pages have become this book.

Allow me to preface this book with one very clear fact: I do not have all the answers. What you are about to read are merely my observations, experiences, and some lessons learned throughout the years. It's an attempt to guide you through the journey of kindergarten. As an educator and a parent, I have so much I'd like to share with you on an extremely important topic: our children. Parenting today is challenging, to say the least. Yet it is the number-one most important job in the world, and it doesn't even come with a manual.

Can you imagine attempting to perform surgery, fixing the engine of a car, or being an accountant without ever having any education in those fields or at least a crash course to prepare you somewhat? Of course not, but that's what parenting is like—figuring it out as you go along, making mistakes and trying not to repeat them. It's not easy. I'm sure every generation before us felt the same way, as will our own children when they finally enter into this phase as well. But let's be honest here: we are up against a lot more nowadays than any other generation before us. My own mother tells me she feels sorry for parents raising children in today's world. The age of technology is moving faster than we can even possibly keep up with. Just when I've talked my oldest out of having a Facebook account, my youngest is on Instagram! They know more than I do about technology, and that is a very scary concept. Cell phones, texting, laptops, Facebook, Twitter, and Vine—I don't even know who is in my own house sometimes with FaceTime! I hear voices of my children's friends in their bedrooms as if they are actually here: "Hey, Mom! Say hi to Dan! Say hi to Becky!" I can't keep up.

We parents are up against more external influences today than ever before. If you are reading this, thinking, *This won't become a big problem for our family; I'll stay right on top of things with my children,* good luck! No one can escape the challenges of raising children with technology. It is and will continue to be part of life as our children know it. I wish I could count how many five- and six-year-olds have brought in their iPod or iPad for show-and-tell. The things they are exposed to or can be influenced by are far out of our reach to some degree. Of course it is our responsibility to monitor what our children are doing, especially when it comes to Internet access, but what is readily available to them without our consent is startling.

So how do we raise decent, kind, well-mannered, and intelligent children? Where do we begin on this journey we call parenthood? In a word—*home.* Everything begins in the home. The examples we set and the things we teach our children will shape who they become and the relationships they will develop and will give them the roots they need to grow and find happiness in their lives. As I have mentioned, I'm a teacher. Teachers tend to blame parents, and parents tend to blame teachers for what we are seeing in today's youth. As I have the wonderful and blessed opportunity of being both teacher and a parent, I say let's stop this now. Let's work *together* and help our children along their path.

Parents and teachers must be a cohesive unit. We are all advocates for the child. We need to remember that we are all on the same team and we all want the same result in the end: to have a happy and successful child.

When we think of success, we need to remember that success isn't necessarily measured just by the report card. Sure, high grades are more than desirable. After all, we now have additional learning centers, both before and after school; math programs over the summer to keep parents from living in fear that their students will be "behind" all the other kids; as well as honors systems starting in many schools as early as the third grade.

When we are talking about the success of the child, we have to think of the whole child—the big picture. Does your child have friends he or she enjoys playing with? Is he involved in some form of sport or physical activity? Does she have hobbies? Is he willing to try new things? Can she use her imagination? Are the children happy? Are they independent? Are they ready to venture out on their own in the school setting? Where can this all come together for your child? In kindergarten. Kindergarten is where *this* all begins.

Most of us have some specific recollections or memories of kindergarten. My husband fell in love at age five with his teacher, Miss Allison. She had red hair. Guess who he married? A redheaded kindergarten teacher. My oldest son remembers meeting his best friend on the first day of school, and they are still best friends to this day. Some recall the classroom, certain toys, or what kind of lunch box they may have had. I remember the playground and the fact that my aunt Jean worked in the school. She brought our milk into the classroom every day. Getting a smile or a wave from her was the highlight of my day.

We may remember being nervous, excited, or scared. This is a big day! After all, there's a lot of buildup to the first day of kindergarten. All summer long, our parents introduce us to people, telling them, "Johnny's going into kindergarten in September!" Or "Guess who Susie's teacher is!" There is always a big conversation between the parents as to which friends their child will be with too. "Oh, you got Mrs. Jones? Great! They will be together then?"

The focus is entirely on the children at this point, but what most of us will never know or remember from our first day of kindergarten is how our parents felt. No one remembers how their mom or dad felt. (In fact, in those days, I don't think there was even one single dad at the school. It was all moms, as far as I can recall. My mom stayed home with the three of us girls, and my dad went to work.) When I stop to think about it, I have never once asked my mom how she felt when she dropped me off. I have no idea if it was emotional for her, being that I was her "baby," or if she did the happy dance because she just unloaded her last kid. Nope, no one thinks of or remembers their parents on this monumental day. No one gives much thought to how they felt or what *they* were going through. So many parents, so many emotions; that I can tell you from a teacher's perspective. Some tear up, many take pictures, and most are anxious. I know—I've been there myself four times. I always got teary-eyed, sometimes took pictures (okay, I forgot my camera by the fourth child), and often felt anxious. Why? Well, for one thing, I felt like I was handing my baby over to a total stranger. (Now that I think of it, I was, in a way.)

After all, here is this person who is going to be spending the better part of her day with my child. All of a sudden, my daughter is drawing pictures with hearts on them for someone else! I admit it—I was a little jealous. I was grateful that she was bonding with this woman and I felt comfortable with her, but I'm only human. Another thing I struggled with was the fact they were now on the school schedule that they would be on for the *rest of their lives*! *This is it? I only get you all to myself for five years?*

It just didn't seem fair. I felt so ripped off. My children went to full-day kindergarten that started and ended just like all of the other grades … I started to wonder if I was really ready for this. Then I remembered something (like a sledgehammer to my head): "Oh, yeah … this isn't about *me*. It's about them." It's about if they were ready to leave me and embark on this new adventure called kindergarten. Guess what—all four of them were more than ready. In fact, most children usually are.

Chapter 2

The Underestimated Importance of Kindergarten

What exactly is kindergarten anyway? Does it exist in other countries around the world? Yes, in fact, it does, although sometimes with different meanings and by different names. For the most part though, kindergarten is defined as an establishment or institution where children between the ages of four and six prepare for the first formal year of education.

Okay, so let's break this down a bit. You may have a four year old entering kindergarten in the United States but his birthday is quickly approaching, and most cutoff dates to enter kindergarten are between October 1 and December 1. Most children are five, turning six, but it varies. I feel the meaning has changed quite a bit over the years—preparing for the first year of formal education? Not so much anymore. Most kindergarten programs actually *are* the first formal year of school, not a preparation for one. Kindergarten is not the finger-painting, block-building classroom of yesteryear. We now have a more formal, state mandated, core curriculum that is to be followed by private and public schools alike. In fact, many school districts throughout the country have kindergarten take part in the standardized testing along with the rest of the school. There are textbooks and workbooks for many, classroom libraries, writing journals, learning centers, and even homework. Kindergarten has become much more of a formal year of education.

As a teacher, I feel as though I'm always trying to find a balance between work and play for the children. My ultimate goal is to incorporate the two into my curriculum. Learning should and can be stimulating—and certainly exciting! There are countless subject areas to cover at this age level, but we need to remember how old the children are. Oftentimes I feel as though I need to make sure the children have sufficient time to actually play! But we all know that learning does not have to only come from a paper and pencil, and at this age it is imperative to make learning hands-on, engaging, creative, and just plain fun. Children will remember a lot more about the life cycle of the butterfly by raising their own butterfly garden in the classroom than by just seeing it in a book. Learning can and should be cooperative and interactive.

Academics in kindergarten consist of language arts (pre-reading and reading, handwriting, phonics, pre-writing and writing) as well as math, science, social studies, and in some cases religious studies. This is all wonderful and of course necessary, but what about learning and developing socially and emotionally? How and when does all this happen? Is there any other grade in the world after kindergarten that actually allows you stop and play together or even talk over a snack together? No, not really … most of these incredible and critical exchanges only take place in kindergarten. There is so much to be learned from each other through free play, board games, outdoor organized games, sports, blocks, Play-Doh, painting, and whatever else you can imagine! These are the moments when the shy little boy may make a new friend, or the assertive girl may have to learn to wait her turn. A child may learn that there is more than one way to build a tower or ask for help when he or she isn't sure how to play Candy Land. Children may learn that when you are playing "house," you don't always get to be the mother.

If you were to walk into my classroom during indoor recess or free play, you would find a classroom full of engaged children with a variety of activities going on. I call it "controlled chaos," or at least that's what it may look like. But do not be fooled. While the children are all engaged in their activity of choice and I am correcting papers or preparing our next lesson, rest assured that as their kindergarten teacher, I am fully and completely aware of who is (or isn't) playing with whom, what they are playing or working on, who helped clean up and who didn't, who is reading to whom, and so on. I watch who pushed in their chair when they were finished at the writing table and who put the markers, crayons, and colored pencils away. I see who went first in a game and who didn't try to quit when things didn't go their way—and on and on and on. These are the priceless and invaluable teaching and learning moments I live for. I promise that your child will know all of his or her academic lesson and be fully prepared for first grade by June. But even more importantly, I can assure the parents that I am teaching, shaping, and molding the future of tomorrow.

As in many schools, informal visiting tours go on throughout the school year. Certain times of the year are certainly busier than others, whether it's the beginning of the year and you have people who just moved to the area or have an open house of sorts. You may even find this more so in many private schools as people are "shopping around" to learn about the different schools and programs in their surrounding town.

Whatever the case may be, I find it fascinating (and secretly quite comical, to be very honest) that whoever is giving the tour, whether it's the principal, another teacher, or the secretary, they breeze by kindergarten if it is clearly not a structured learning time. The noise (which doesn't bother me; they are children) or the varied activities seem to almost embarrass them to the point that they feel the need to explain what's going on and reassure our visitor that free play is almost over and instruction will soon begin again. It is at this time that I am called over to explain what they are witnessing and go over our academic curriculum.

I remember a visitor with a member of our administration popping in. The children were working with partners. Each pair was body tracing his or her partner for our particular exercise. The administrator actually tried to make a quick exit so as to not expose the potential new parent to the lack of structure the parent was witnessing! It wasn't terribly noisy, and everyone was quite busy. Do you know what they were actually witnessing? Turn taking, shared learning experiences, working with partners—learning through a hands-on activity—children having fun in school! Sounds like a perfect recipe for success to me.

Before my visitors could get away, I invited them in to see these amazing young people at work with original and creative ideas of their own. I invited the children to explain to the adults what they were doing. One little girl said it best: "We're learning what's so special about each other!" and they did learn what was so very special about each other. When the tracing and cutting was done, the partners had to look at each other and draw and color what kind of hair the partner had, what color eyes, if he or she wore glasses, had pierced ears, and whatever other details that made the partner unique. They had a blast doing this activity and learned a little bit more about a fellow classmate that day.

When they completed their project, each pair presented their final product to the class and described one another and told us one thing that made that person special. We hung those beautiful body tracings high on the walls that day and left them up for the whole year. Week after week, I would hear the children talk to each other and laugh at how funny their hair came out or how pretty their friend drew a hair bow on them. So there in the midst of my "controlled chaos" my students made a new friend, worked together, and felt proud. There is no greater lesson. That visitor wound up sending her children to our school the following year, and she later told me how taken she was with what she witnessed that day in my classroom. What she witnessed was the magic and pure joy of kindergarten.

Kindergarten is unique from any other grade. It's always interesting to me when someone asks me what I do for a living; it is the exact same conversation *every single* time. Here's how it goes. I tell them I'm a teacher. Then they ask me what grade I teach and I tell them kindergarten. "Kindergarten? How adorable! That's sweet. That must be a lot of fun!"

Adorable? Sweet? Fun? Oh sure, kindergarten is all of those things, but trust me ... it is so much more. I have often felt that the importance and significance of kindergarten is severely underestimated in the United States. We still have countless school districts throughout the country that do not even offer a full-day program. I have taught from kindergarten through eighth grade in public, private, and parochial schools, and believe me, teaching kindergarten is not for everyone.

Some of my own colleagues have made jokes over the years, telling me, "You're crazy! You really should have your head examined—how can you do this all day?"

It takes a pretty thick skin to be asked questions like that and not get too insulted. I'm not going to lie—I feel somewhat dismissed and not as professionally viewed by many fellow educators. Let's be honest. Teaching eighth-grade algebra sounds just a little bit more intellectual than teaching kindergarten, don't you think? After all, the older students are preparing for high school, and that's a heavy responsibility for those teachers.

But if you stop to think about it, we all have to start somewhere, don't we? If kindergarten is so cute and adorable, then why don't we just send those little cuties from pre-K straight to first grade and see what happens? It would be a disaster—a total and complete mess.

Last year I was having a conversation with three other women, all highly intelligent and very successful in their prospective careers. One is a high-powered business executive who works for a pharmaceutical company and travels the world. The other two women are nurses—or "über nurses," as the high-powered executive referred to them (although in my personal opinion, every nurse is an über nurse!). One of these nurses is the head of a very large trauma facility, and the other works for one of the most prestigious research hospitals in the United States. These women are extremely smart, ambitious, and capable. As I sat and listened to their conversation about finding cures for certain diseases and breakthroughs on the drugs, finally someone asked me, "What do you do for a living?," and, as it happens 99 percent of the time, I got the same reply I usually do—you know—the one I had previously mentioned.

Not only did I attend the same prestigious university as these three women and have a college degree just like they have, I was the only one sitting at the table that held a master's degree. I am certified in two different states to teach up to the eighth grade. Now, my feelings on this reaction are not at all reflective on how I feel about my career choice. They are a reflection on what adults—parents and professionals included—think about the value of kindergarten.

You know what? Big mistake. Huge. Kindergarten is the gateway to your child's educational experience. It was interesting how the conversation quickly turned from "cute" to what their own children's kindergarten experiences were—two of them were horrific, complete with having a child sit *under* a chair as a punishment for "bad" behavior, and the other one was told that something was seriously wrong with her son for preferring to play with girls! I asked if either of these teachers had been arrested for their negligence (okay—maybe a bit severe, but my blood pressure was rising at the thought of both teachers' inexcusable actions).

If your child has a negative experience, for whatever reason— good luck getting him or her excited for first grade. If children aren't given the academic basics, reading could be that much more difficult for them. If they aren't given the proper opportunity to socialize and make friendships, it could be challenging to connect with other children in their class. If they don't feel safe to explore, learn, and make mistakes in a caring, safe, and loving environment, this could hinder their self-esteem and confidence for years to come. This is not to say they are in danger of a failed academic career, but I can assure you that with a rich, stimulating, and positive kindergarten experience, your children are on the path to academic success as well as loving school.

As the teacher who is responsible for ensuring this happens for each and every student who comes through my door, I feel blessed and honored to be at the helm of this amazing journey. I always tell my parents that I have two goals for their children. First is for them to *want* to come to school—every day. No tears— just enthusiasm, excitement, and wonder; that's all you need. My second goal is to have them prepared for first grade by the end of the year. Everything else in between will fall into place. How lucky am I to be the one to show these children the way? Kindergarten is as special and amazing for me as I hope it is for them. Kindergarten has always been and, I suspect, always will be my first love.

There is something absolutely magical about five-year-olds who are embarking on the amazing journey. They are so innocent, pure, impressionable, and honest. They are at an incredible stage in their lives—so young, yet so ready. They are ready to become independent thinkers. They are about to spread their wings a little bit—choose their own friends, be responsible for their own belongings, remember their manners without a reminder, display self-control on their own.

The beauty of this stage is that children have yet to be overly influenced by outside forces, somewhat unaware of the skepticism of the real world. They don't base friendships on monetary status, ethnic similarities, or even gender. They don't care who you are or what you look like. As long as you are somewhat kind to them and willing to play—you're in! Best friends in record time—I love it.

Children nowadays begin kindergarten with so many different prior experiences. Some have gone to part-time preschool programs, some have gone to full-day programs, and many have been in day care since birth. Some have had no formal school setting experience at all. This means the experience has been different for the parents as well. Some parents work full-time, part-time, or have two working parents outside the home; some have stay-at-home moms or even stay-at-home dads. There are many children who have come to me over the years from a divorced home or one in the process of divorce. There have also been a few with a terminally ill parent or who have already lost a parent. We don't know what goes on in other people's homes or what their experience has been.

That being said, this is the perfect time to get to know the other families because you are about to share in a very important experience together. Ultimately, we are all raising our children together.

Chapter 3

Leading Up to the "Big Day"

So what exactly goes on leading up to the "big day"—the first day of kindergarten? Shopping for clothes, shoes, school supplies, a lunch box, and a backpack, calming possible fears, sharing in excitement, trying to get back on a reasonable bedtime schedule after a carefree summer—the list goes on.

Many schools will send home a letter at some point over the summer. This letter should have all of the pertinent information you need for your child to start school. It will probably tell you the exact first day of school and the hours of the first week. Be aware that the first week more often than not has different or shortened hours. Pay close attention so you know the schedule, which will reduce the chance for any unwanted stress for you or your child. If you are a working parent, you'll want to find this out as soon as possible if you want to adjust your work schedule, especially for the first day. In many cases you can even call the school's main office in June before your child begins kindergarten, as the school calendar is usually made up that far in advance. It never hurts to think ahead.

Many schools will also send home a supply list in advance to tell what school supplies your child will need. Some teachers are very specific and some teachers do not have as much of a preference. If your child's kindergarten teacher lists that the child should have a standard eight-by-ten plastic supply box, do not go out and get them a sixteen by twenty. This is not a time to think bigger is better. Many times certain requests are the result of spacing and storage issues, and you should try your best to adhere to the requests made by the teacher. If the teacher is requesting an eight-count box of crayons, do not go out and buy a box of sixty-four! Very often the classroom has additional supplies, or very simply, that is all the teacher feels your child needs.

Most children cannot wait to pick out their backpack and lunch box—I can't blame them. This is exciting stuff! I mean, really. Superman, princesses, Thomas the Tank Engine, My Little Pony—where does one begin? When my oldest son was starting school, I could not wait to help him pick out his backpack. He decided on Batman. I was so excited to order his backpack online that I wanted to be 100 percent sure I ordered it properly. (Keep in mind that this was the first thing I had ever ordered online before in my entire life.) So I placed the order and hit the send button. I wanted to be really sure it went through, so I thought I should just hit send one more time. There was no way I was disappointing this kid, so just to be extra sure I hit it again … okay, twice. Well, the good news is, he wasn't disappointed! The backpack finally came. Then another one came and another and then one more.

My kids still love to bring that story up when they see me shopping online. Let's just say my husband sat me down at the keyboard and gave the teacher a lesson on how *not* to hit send more than once. Lesson learned!

Lunch boxes are another thing to think about—make sure it's what you need if you like to send icepacks with their lunches (my kids never requested one and I never offered). If your child's lunch requires utensils, make sure there's room (and don't forget to send them if they need one!). I can't tell you how many thermoses of mac and cheese I've seen come in without a utensil, and not all teachers have that accessible.

In some schools, kindergarten will eat lunch in the main cafeteria with the rest of the school. Others offer lunch right in the class room. Whatever the case may be, be sure to send in all the necessary items for your child to eat lunch. You should have a conversation with your child about what you would like to send for him or her or order for lunch. I'm not saying take special orders or play restaurant every day. Chances are you'll be making lunches at night while your child is sleeping or putting it together in the morning during the start of the day's craziness. But you should be aware of what your child can or cannot open on his or her own, how much the child eats, what he or she likes to drink. Show your children which part to eat first (cookies shouldn't be first but often are if you're not watching!), etc.

Without fail, every year I have students sadly tell me, with tears in their eyes, "I don't like what Mommy packed me." At this point there is not a lot I can do to make them feel better, and I certainly can't offer them an alternative. I'm not sure why some students seem surprised with what's in their lunch box—maybe they just like what the person next to them has better—but it's often a good idea to know what they are willing to eat and what they won't. There has been many a kindergartner who has tried to slink up to the garbage can with a Ziploc bag full of perfect, beautiful strawberries or an unopened yogurt who tried to toss them in before I catch them. When busted—as they usually are—I remind them how their parents thought this was a healthy choice and that they are so lucky to have such a wonderful lunch prepared for them. If it is something they really don't like, then they need to discuss it with their parents, but for today, I tell them, this is what you are eating. (Never once have I seen a parent pack something his or her child has never had before, no matter how much a five year old tries to convince me otherwise.)

Similarly, if your school offers a hot lunch program, let your child be in on the decision-making process when selecting the meal. This way he or she knows what to expect, and you can be sure your child is going to eat what you ordered. This way the child is not wasting food and you are not wasting your money.

Let's move on to school clothing. Many private and parochial schools require a uniform. It has become my understanding that there is a new movement in certain parts of the country that some public schools are going this route as well. If your school requires your child to be in uniform, here are a few tips.

First, do *not* wait until the third week of August to go to your local uniform store! It's a zoo—total and complete anarchy! It's not even safe—trust me, I am speaking from experience. With my first son I waited until school was about to start because I was convinced that he was going to grow six inches over the summer and thought it was best to wait. When we went to the uniform store and had to wait on the very, very long line, I vowed to never do that again. At the young age of a kindergartner, those little uniforms have elastic in the waist and plenty of hem room for them to grow.

Be smart and go over the summer when no one else is thinking about uniform shopping and the store is empty. This way they have your size and a much less cranky sales clerk. The next thing about a uniform is that it is just that—uniform. The word *uniform* by definition means identical or consistent, without variation from example to example. So if your school requires navy socks with a skirt, do not send your daughter in white. If it requires black shoes, do not send your son in his favorite Nike high-tops. Familiarize yourself with the proper uniform and dress code and respect it. Deviating from it with no regard sends the wrong message to your child on many levels. Not to mention you could be avoiding a note home or an unwanted phone call from the school. If your child is in a school without a uniform, I would bet that there is still some form of a dress code in which you are to comply. If it is not listed on any letters sent home over the summer, it will be most likely posted on your school's website. You should check it out.

If there is no uniform and your child is free to wear whatever you choose, remember that he or she is going to kindergarten. Children will be getting dirty, playing outside, making projects, and possibly using art supplies. A smock can only cover so much. Don't spend a fortune on fancy outfits or designer clothes. If you send your children to school in Uggs or expensive sneakers, please remember that they will come home a little worse for the wear. I'm often saddened when I open my door for children to see their parents after six or seven hours of school, and the first thing I hear is, "What's all over your shirt?"

How about, "Well, you look like you had fun!" or "Wow! What exciting things did you do in school today?" I have had parents come up to me asking if their child hit her head and why didn't they get a phone call. (It was merely pink sidewalk chalk on her skin.). Or asking how to get the paint out of their child's pants. Parents please believe me when I tell you, clothes can go in the washer and stains can be removed, but the memory of a great day in school with a new friend or an awesome project that has your child excited about learning ... that is the great stuff that lasts forever. Cherish it, and don't sweat the small stuff like stains (because in kindergarten, whatever it is is probably washable anyway!).

As a teacher, I give a lot of thought to how the parents are feeling, as well as the children. Every year, without fail, I have a parent or two pull me aside on the first day of school to let me know a little something about his or her child that the parent feels is pertinent information I need to know: "Michael is very shy and may start to cry when we leave," "Thomas is my 'wanderer'—please keep an eye on him," "You should know, Mrs. Podest, Mary can read"—I love this one—"she's been reading since she was four and also knows her times tables."

This is my signal that it's time for the parents to leave. I don't mean this in a harsh or dismissive way at all—not by any stretch. I know there will be parents who are sitting by the phone at home or at work waiting for a call "in case of emergency." I have seen the parents fighting back tears or the parents who leave with tears rolling down their cheeks. I've seen the parents who are certain their child will not be okay—when in turn the child is fine and it's the parents feeling the pain.

We worry that our children may be afraid to ask to use the bathroom, may not be able to open their thermos without our help, or may not make a friend. These are all completely normal concerns; after all, we're parents! Worrying about our kids is what we do best! The good news is I have never had one child *not* make it through their first day. Not one. In fact, they very often surprise everyone and do beautifully. We tend to underestimate these little people.

Now I am as guilty as any other parent of worrying about my kids. It's only out of our deep love for our children that we behave this way. But we are not giving them enough credit for what they are capable of. Year after year I am blown away by these amazing little human beings and what they can do, given the opportunity. As I said, I'm guilty of enabling too—I'll tie my son's shoes because it's faster for me to do it, I'll fold and hang up their clothes because I can do it better—or worse, I can do it "right"! I've even been known to pack up their things for them because heaven forbid they forget something they can't possibly live without. Kindergarten is the ideal time to start having a little more faith in what our children can do on their own—but we must provide the opportunities for them to succeed and give them a little space when they don't.

The first day of school is a very special day, and the classroom is always filled with excitement! There's the hustle and bustle of people coming and going—moms, dads, and siblings coming in to see the decorated classroom, help their children find their designated hook in the closet or maybe a cubby with their name on it. There is joy yet trepidation for many. This is the time to have more confidence in your children than ever before. Whether you realize it or not, you have been preparing them for this very moment for five years. You have cared for them, loved them, and given them all of the tools they need to go off on their own. It isn't always easy for us as parents to let go, but it is imperative to our children's growth and personal development. There is no greater gift that we can give our children than showing our faith and confidence in them. We certainly do it on the ball field, don't we? We aren't out there on the soccer field with them or in the dance recital beside them, are we? No—we are on the sidelines cheering them on, celebrating their success, and consoling them when they feel defeated. We need to serve them the same way in school and we should begin that as early as kindergarten.

I had a little girl one year who had difficulty coming to school each day. She was very anxious and struggled with new situations and transitional change. Every day from September through December the mom would painstakingly walk her distraught and crying daughter into the classroom. I could see the anguish on the mother's face as she felt bad for her daughter but had to get to work. The poor child would cry so hard that she would have trouble breathing and proceeded to beg her mom not to leave. This went on day after day for months.

All the other children came into the classroom each morning on their own. They either came in off the bus or their parents had dropped them curbside, where we had an "ambassador system" of volunteering parents and upper-grade students who were responsible for getting the younger students out of the car and overseeing them to their classroom door.

I had suggested to the mom of this little girl to pull up curbside as well and let the ambassadors take over from there. She didn't feel that this would be best for her daughter and claimed it would take her more time to get on this line of cars, thus making her even later for work. I informed her that it would in fact be quicker for her to drop her off and assured her I would be ready and waiting for her crying daughter every morning. I promised that we would figure this out together and that I was more than happy to handle this situation.

To no avail—this was how she wanted to proceed, so I decided to back off. I waited. I knew this couldn't go on like this forever. Parent–teacher conference time came in early December, and the girl's parents came in to see me for a visit. Once more I proposed to the parents to drop the child off like every other child in the class was doing and that I would take care of everything from there. There was definite resistance, and I was sensing some hostility by the mother at my persistence.

She finally said to me, "This is our little thing that we do together and I *like* to walk her in. I like to see her get settled in, and truthfully, I want to be sure none of the other kids are making fun of her for crying." There it was. This wasn't about the child's anxieties nearly as much as it was about the mom's.

Why do we underestimate our children in certain situations? They are so much more capable and able than we realize and have an amazing capacity to adapt to many different situations.

I kindly told the mom that this wasn't helping her daughter to adjust to kindergarten or to our morning routine. The other students were walking themselves in every day, greeting me on their own, hanging up and putting away their things, and I knew she could do it as well. I also informed her that not only wasn't anyone making fun of her daughter but the other students were all ready each day to do what they could to help her daughter feel better. I was touched each morning witnessing pure empathy and compassion at such a young age.

I asked the mom one last time—actually, I pleaded with her. Please drop her off at the curb regardless of any resistance she got from her child. Don't make it a big deal. Just let her know the next morning that it was time for her to walk herself in. I told her to tell her daughter how proud she was of her and that she knew she could do it.

So the next day came and who came in all on her own ... but my little girl who had cried for months. Yes, she had tears in her eyes, but she did it! She walked through that door all on her own! I was so deeply proud of her courage as I know that this was not easy for her. The other students even noticed and showered the little girl with praise and hugs.

As I have said before, it is our job to have faith and confidence in what our children can accomplish on their own. It is also our responsibility to provide the opportunity for them to be independent and successful. I was as proud of the mom that day as I was of her daughter—they had both learned a little something about themselves and about each other.

Chapter 4

Welcome to the Melting Pot

As your child begins on his or her journey through school, so do you, the parents. There is a lot for us to navigate, especially if this is your first child attending kindergarten or if you are starting in a new school. Maybe you've moved and are new to the town or city you live in. At any rate, there is so much for parents to learn and figure out as well.

When a child begins kindergarten in any school, there are a few very important things to keep in mind. You are about to meet the families that your child will be interacting with and sharing life experiences with for quite some time. "Families," as we know, come in all different shapes, sizes, and colors nowadays. You are going to meet many single parents, whether it's through divorce or death. You are going to meet families where the grandparents are an essential part of the child's upbringing and may be the one you see at pick up or for playdates. You are going to come across different family dynamics—firstborn children, only children, families with new babies, large families, small families, families with much older siblings, or "half" siblings, also known as "stepbrothers" or "stepsisters." You may meet families from different ethnic backgrounds or with different religious beliefs.

This is an ideal time to teach your children about acceptance and to enable them to broaden their spectrum.

Regardless of where you live or what type of school your child attends, you will not meet one other family that is exactly like your own—not one. You may share similar beliefs, values, and morals, but ultimately each family is unique unto themselves. It is our responsibility to teach our children at this tender age to embrace each other's differences. This is how we learn—we learn from each other. I've often said to my own kids, wouldn't it be so boring if the whole world was made up of the exact same kind of person? Isn't life so much more interesting because we are all different from each other?

When my oldest son started preschool, he came home day after day talking about a new friend that he had made. He told me they would play blocks together and go on the jungle gym together. They also shared a love of dinosaurs—they were a match made in heaven!

One day I asked my son what his friend's name was and he told me it was Henri. What kind of a name was this? I wondered. I thought he must have misunderstood his friend and decided to seek out the boy and his mother at dismissal in the hopes of setting up a playdate. When my son pointed them out, there was Henri and his mom. His mother was also looking for my son as she had a lollipop that she wanted to give him. She wanted to say thank you to my son for helping her son learn his first English words. What my son never told me was that Henri had just moved to the United States from Lebanon and didn't speak English. His family only spoke Arabic at home. I had no idea. How were these boys playing together day after day without communicating in English? How could they express to each other how much they enjoyed each other's company? Didn't they realize how different they were from each other? How they spoke, what they ate, how they dressed. Nope—none of that mattered. Not to them. All they saw was a friend—someone who made them happy and made them feel good about coming to school. These two boys went on to have playdates throughout the year, and Henri started to learn more English. It was so heartwarming to see how these two little boys looked out for each other and reveled in each other's differences. There was no milk and cookies at Henri's house after school—my son came home having just tried tabbouleh and Lebanese custard! I remember seeing the two of them stuffed into a recliner chair watching *The Land before Time* movies, laughing themselves silly. They were the perfect example of pure acceptance and friendship—and they were happy. I also got to know Henri's mother, who was the most lovely, warm lady I had met at the school that year. They later moved to Florida, and my son was sad to see his friend go. But neither of us ever forgot the lessons learned that year, and they didn't come from a schoolbook—they came from the heart.

When our children begin school, it is important to listen to them—I mean really listen. We don't need to "grill" them on every move they made in school that day, but ask thoughtful questions so they open up to you and share their day. It has been my experience that these conversations often arise in the car (turn the radio off), at bath time, or at bedtime. For some reason, children have a lot to share at bedtime (maybe they're trying to prolong the inevitable) and will often tell you something that is on their mind. Be specific in your questions, as children this age are extremely literal. You may want to ask what toys they played with during playtime or if they spent time with anyone new that day. Also realize that they can go for months and months without knowing their "best friend's" name simply because it doesn't really matter to them. They will, however, tell you that "she has yellow hair" of that "he's really good on the monkey bars!" Have them show you in their class picture who they like to play with, or have them point a child out to you at school dismissal. They know who they feel comfortable with and who they enjoy spending time with—let them lead the way.

It is always appropriate to ask the teacher for some input in regard to playdates or fostering friendships. Your children's teacher is really the only person who knows your children in school. I can't say I *really* know my own children in school—I've never taught them in school. The children's classroom is *their* world. They are making decisions on their own now—Should I raise my hand to answer a question? Is this a good time to use the bathroom? Should I play with the boy who keeps asking me to play tag?

Ultimately they may be choosing some new friends without your supervision or direction. This is where the teacher comes in. I thoughtfully observe my students on the playground and in the classroom to see who they are interacting with and how they are interacting. Is one person clearly the leader and the other more of a follower? Is one shy and the other outgoing? Is one very mature and the other a little less mature? I often find it amusing and amazing, the pairing off or the little groups of friends that form. Sometimes certain children are drawn to children similar to themselves, which is what most people would expect. And then there are other times that "Felix and Oscar" rear their funny little heads—I call them the Odd Couple—the most unlikely of pairs yet a pair that makes perfect sense when you think about it.

I once had two little boys in my class who could not have been more different from each other! They came from entirely different ethnic backgrounds and were both first generation, so their cultures were very strong and prevalent in every aspect of their lives. Both boys spoke other languages in the home and ate ethnic food even in school. But the biggest difference between these two boys was intellectually. One of the boys was extremely bright and well beyond his years in maturity as well as in his aptitude for learning. He behaved more like a second-grader and read like a third-grader. The other boy had never even been in school before, did not know his letters, and had learning disabilities (we later discovered) that affected his performance in school.

The more mature one seemed to notice the other boy struggling to complete an activity, assignment, or project. Whenever he would complete his work, he would ask if he could go help the boy in need. I was always so touched by this genuine friendship that developed and saw in the end that they were actually filling a need for each other. It was sweet and innocent. They were the oddest of pairs, yet watching them play and work together made perfect sense. They had become the best of friends. Thankfully both sets of parents listened to their respective sons and allowed them time to get together outside of school—meeting up at the park, playdates, etc. The parents listened and followed their lead, and in the end the two families established a nice bond as well.

I can remember sitting at a parent–teacher conference one time with a mother discussing her child's progress. The mother herself was an Ivy League scholar and a self-proclaimed overachiever. Her daughter, at this very young age, seemed like she may have been heading in her mother's footsteps. Her daughter was reading on a third-grade level, went to Kumon math (an after-school math and reading program) three days a week (after attending full-day kindergarten from 8:00 a.m. to 2:00 p.m.), took Spanish lessons, and played piano well beyond her years. This was all very impressive as this little girl was clearly juggling many different tasks that required so much time and dedication. When I asked who her daughter was playing with after school or on the weekends, the mother told me they haven't gotten around to that yet. The little girl was so busy she didn't have time to *play*! Is there something wrong with this picture? I think so.

While it is absolutely admirable to expose our children to culture, sports, music, advanced academics, etc., we must remember that they are, in fact, children. They need time to play. They need a healthy balance of work and play from an early age. You know your own children better than anyone. Know their strengths, weaknesses, interests, and limitations. In this crazy, busy world we all live in, be sure to schedule "playtime" for your children with a friend. Put it on the calendar in advance if you have to with other parents. Make a date at the park, invite someone over—just be sure to make it happen. Playtime is so important at this age (actually, at every age. Make some playtime for yourself too!).

One of my favorite poems in the world was written by Robert Fulgham: "All I Really Need to Know I Learned in Kindergarten." It's about life's most simple yet imperative lessons that are learned in kindergarten and are applicable our whole lives through. Think about it in the adult world that you live in—your profession, your circle of friends, your church or place of worship, your community. Do you play fair? Clean up your own mess? Put things back where you found them? How many times do we blame others when things don't go our way? How often do we point the finger and only think of serving ourselves verses the greater good?

These simple yet prophetic thoughts should resonate and permeate every single person, every single day. Ah ... what a wonderful world it would be (do you hear Louis Armstrong singing?). Did you ever stop to think that kindergarten is the place where not only are you learning to read and write, you are learning about the person you will become? There are so few times throughout one's life when we are given the time or the opportunity to develop and grow personally and intrinsically without tremendous pressure from the outside world or under a microscope. Five- and six-year-old children don't stress about memorizing their sight words or knowing basic math facts, their parents do! Nope, children this age just want to have fun, be engaged, and make a friend or two. It is the kindergarten teacher's job and responsibility to make sure this happens in a very natural, safe, and secure environment.

I *love* the last line in this poem: "Be aware of wonder." Watch out! You might learn something here! I was always one of those students who probably drove the teachers a little bit crazy with the amount of questions I asked in school. I can remember my mom telling me that the only stupid question is the one that goes unasked. So there it was—permission from my own mother to fire away. I can remember my second-grade teacher who scolded me when I pointed out that she misspelled something on the board—"*Don't you ever correct an adult!*"

What? But she spelled the word wrong. Not only did she scare and embarrass me that day, I never understood why what I did was so wrong.

My son had a similar experience one year, and it will probably stay with him forever, as my experience has stayed with me. My son is extremely hard-working, bright, and efficient. If he does not understand something or is unsure of something, he will not rest until he clarifies what is puzzling or confusing him. Personally, I find this to be an extremely admirable trait and one that will always serve him well in life. (Of course I do—he gets it from me!)

Sadly, his teacher at the time didn't look at things quite the same way. When my son raised his hand and pressed on about a question he had, his teacher said in front of the class, "You know what? You really get on my nerves with all the questions you ask. Put your hand down."

My son came home from school that day a different child. His face was purple with embarrassment, mortified at how he was made to feel in front of his classmates, and he had never known his teacher felt that way about him. What had he been taught? He learned not to ask too many questions, not to be curious, not to wonder. Shame on that teacher.

Thankfully, by the next day the teacher approached me to ask if she could speak to my son to apologize—apparently she'd had trouble sleeping because of the way she had treated her student. While I appreciated that she reflected on the effect of her words and her actions, it was too little, too late. The damage was done. I took this as an opportunity to teach my son that people do make mistakes and when someone is truly genuinely sorry for hurting you, you need to forgive and move on. He moved on and we got past it, but I'm not going to lie—I never quite looked at that teacher the same way again.

When my students catch an error of mine, I always take the opportunity to laugh at myself, praise them for their astuteness, and remind them that no one is perfect—not even the "almighty adult." They know from day one that my classroom is the safest place in the world to ask questions, make mistakes, and take risks. No one is going to scold you or laugh at you—no way! In my classroom, we are going to catch each other when we fall and support each other when we need to. No one—child or adult—should ever stop asking questions in life. I am learning every single day of my life. I'm constantly reading different books or surrounding myself with inquisitive, bright, positive people from whom I learn something new.

Open my mind and broaden my horizons ... we should all do this at every age. After all, life is a journey and childhood is a journey too—not a race. Never ever stop wondering. In the words of the great poet Robert Fulgham, "Be aware of wonder. It will take you to great places!"

Chapter 5

Measuring Up

We all love our children more than words can ever say and we want what's best for them, right? But we can't help but worry just a teensy bit about whether our child is "on par" with their new classmates. It is human nature to inquire about what other children the same age are doing, whether it's if they can read or not or what sports they are playing. We want them to be successful and reach their full potential in school and in life. So we do whatever we can to make this happen.

Unfortunately, we don't always give our children enough credit on how they might perform or handle themselves in certain situations. We want to protect them from failure or making mistakes. But I have always thought we learn so much about ourselves and the world around us when we do mess up. It's what we do from there that really defines who we are. So what if children are not given that opportunity? What if we shield them and protect them from any possibility of failure? Then I'm afraid we don't really find out who they can be.

I've met parents whose children were going to be in my class in the upcoming school year and they try to warn me about what's to come with their own child: "Oh, just you wait, Mrs. Podest! This one will give you a run for your money!" or "She doesn't know all of her letters yet and can't read at all!" When did we get a letter stating that reading and/or perfection was a prerequisite for kindergarten?

I was at a party one summer and was having a conversation with two other women—one who is a teacher and one who was a stay-at-home mom with a daughter going into kindergarten that following September. The teacher was telling us she was currently tutoring a boy four times a week—he was starting kindergarten in September. The look on the other woman's face spoke volumes: *Oh no! Should I be doing that with my daughter? My husband and I have discussed it before but then we never did anything about it— she's going to be so behind!*

I felt so sorry for this mother that she would feel this way (and this wasn't even her first child, so she already had some experience). I'm going to let a little secret out of the bag right now and hopefully put all of you moms and dads at ease. Does your child meet the state requirement to be five by a certain date? (This occurs in every state that by a certain date the child must turn five to enter kindergarten.) If so, then short of any serious conditions that might inhibit your child from performing in a formalized classroom setting, he or she is probably ready! When are we going to accept our children for who they are and see all the greatness in their tiny little beings? There is not one classroom in the world that has the makeup of twenty identical students—they are all different! And thank God for that, as variety is the spice of life. I question the current trend where parents are holding their children back on their own accord without any legitimate need or merit. In any given classroom all across America (and the world, for that matter), someone is going to be the youngest student and someone is going to be the oldest. When did it become acceptable for parents to make this decision? We are manipulating the makeup and chemistry of the class by allowing this ever-growing practice. There are children in the same kindergarten class who are sixteen to eighteen months apart in age because a child was held back simply because he was a boy (and we all know boys don't develop as fast as girls, right? Wink, wink!) or because he was a "late birthday"—meaning close to the cutoff date.

I happen to have a son who is a "late birthday," so to speak. It never once occurred to me to hold him back—not as a mother or as a teacher. One day we were at his tee ball game. Now most sports in our town are arranged by your grade, but the baseball program is designed by your age. So because my son was not five by July 1 he had to wait another year to start playing ball. This means he was playing ball with boys who were a grade and sometimes even two behind him. My son also happens to be a big boy and is often perceived to be older than he actually is.

When my son was up to bat, I heard two parents saying, "How old is that boy?"

I told them he missed the cutoff by twenty-three days.

Another mom asked what grade he was in, so I told her. As it turned out, her son had the exact same birthday as mine but she held him back a year in school. It started this whole conversation with people I didn't even know and suddenly I felt under attack!

"Why didn't you hold him back? After all, he's a boy and so close to the cutoff!" One mother told me that's what she did with her older son and it was the best decision she ever made. School was so easy for him, and he was better than everyone else in sports because he was that much older. These parents who were questioning—or should I say grilling—me did not even know that I was a teacher or that my son happened to be the youngest of four. I was pretty comfortable with my decision and certainly did not feel the need to explain myself to strangers.

Why didn't I hold my son back? Because there was absolutely no reason to. Why on earth would I hold him back? Think of that term anyway: "holding them back"—it sounds like it's against their will or like something that isn't natural. Holding my son back would mean, to me, keeping him from the place he should be in.

Like I said before, someone's got to be the youngest. You also have to remember that we have absolutely no way of knowing where all the other children's birthdays are going to fall, so you don't even know what you are up against!

One of my daughters has what is considered an early birthday, which should make her one of the oldest in her grade. Ironically, she happened to be in class with quite a few other boys and girls who also have early birthdays, which puts her closer to the average age. I always thought she would be the oldest and was 100 percent wrong. The cutoff in our district is October 1, which states that any child entering kindergarten needs to turn five by October 1.

When my oldest child was in kindergarten I was preparing to throw his birthday party. He was born in March so he was turning six. It suddenly occurred to me that he hadn't been to many birthday parties. Oh no! Was he not making friends? Was he not getting invited to other children's birthday parties? So I did what any rational and secure first-time mother would do. I took out that class list to see just who these little snots were who were excluding my son! I was going to go through each name one by one and see when *their* birthdays were and count up just how many had left him out! (Okay, I'm exaggerating just a little here ... but not much.) How dare they?

And then it occurred to me ... no one had left him out. He was one of the oldest in the class with a March birthday. This is pretty unusual but it happens. (I silently apologized to all of those little cherubs and their parents.) The majority of students in his grade were summer birthdays. So my point is this—we don't know when the other children's birthdays will be to determine if our child will older or younger. I think it is a huge disservice to try to micromanage and manipulate what grade our children should be in or if they are ready to start kindergarten based solely on the day they were born.

I've met people who were holding newborns telling me they already decided they were going to hold the child back because of when they were born. I don't mean to judge people, and certainly a parent knows their children better than anyone, but would you let a registered nurse change the brakes in your car? Would you let an investment banker do the electrical work in your house? So why are parents taking it upon themselves to make an educational decision? One that is mandated by the district and should not be played with, in my opinion. Parents need to trust in the expertise and opinion of their children's teachers and have faith they will make the best decision for them. As I said, aside from any significant situation, problem, diagnosis, or condition that has obviously been addressed by either a doctor, previous teachers, or professionals in the educational or medical field, children should begin school when they are supposed to begin school.

My first year teaching kindergarten was very exciting. I was newly married and had just secured a teaching job within the public school system—big score! The children in my class were from all walks of life—Greek, Hispanic, Italian, Korean, Japanese, you name it.

I had this one little girl in my class who was just beautiful—let's call her Mary. She was a petite little girl and was very bright. Her birthday was approaching, as I well knew because we had a birthday chart in our classroom. (Birthdays are a huge deal in kindergarten—right up there with losing a tooth!)

So the big day comes and Mary comes into school beyond excited. She had cupcakes for the whole class, and a birthday crown was waiting for her at her seat. As the day went on, she came up to me and told me she had a secret.

"A secret? What is it? I love secrets!"

Mary told me that today she turned five!

I said to her, "No, Mary, today you turned six! You were five already, silly!"

No, she told me, she was five and she was sure of it. In fact, she was so sure because Mommy and Daddy made her promise not to tell anyone that she was indeed really five. Mary seemed very sure about what she was saying. I started to think … she was a little smaller than the other children, but that doesn't mean much. Why would she say this? Or more importantly, why would a child make this up?

As the day went on, this conversation perplexed me. When I had a free moment I went up to the see the school nurse and requested Mary's medical records so I could check on her birth date. There it was right in front of me—Mary was telling the truth. She had indeed turned five on this particular birthday. What was the problem with that? The problem was that the cutoff for the state was October 1, meaning she needed to be five on or before October 1 in order to enter kindergarten. We were in the first week of December at this point. Somehow she slipped in through the system and no one ever noticed. Now what was I to do with this information? I was new to the school and the school district for that matter. I didn't want to get anyone in trouble, but more importantly, I was worried about Mary. What would happen to her down the road? Would she be able to keep up academically? Would she be mature enough being that she would clearly, always be the youngest in the entire grade?

I was a nervous wreck and wasn't sure how to handle this. I had a very nice working relationship with my principal at the time and felt I couldn't keep this to myself. Not only did I not want to do a long-term disservice to Mary, I was worried that somehow this could come back to me that I did not pick up on this (which was never the case but I was a newbie, "low man on the totem pole," and a nervous wreck!). As it turned out this became a pretty big deal. The parents were addressed, as they clearly knew she was too young and did not make the cutoff date although they claimed they didn't realize, as Mary was their first child. This whole case went before a board and became a legal issue. This lasted the whole year, and I hated the tension I felt from Mary's parents when I saw them every day at dismissal. They probably felt like I blew their cover and turned them in, but what they did was wrong. It was wrong to put their daughter in that situation—a situation that could affect her throughout her whole life in school.

I think both parents had to work and had another baby on the way. Their intention was probably that they thought Mary was bright enough and only missed the cut off by a few weeks, so let's give this a shot and see what happens. In the end, after a whole school year of investigating the situation, Mary was permitted to stay in the grade she was in. Ultimately the school district made the error and had missed the birth date. The parents never lied; they wrote down the real year that she was born in, so the board let her stay.

Mary had a great year and progressed beautifully. However, it would have been a much more memorable year for everyone if we weren't dealing with this situation and had this looming over our heads every time we saw each other. This was a case of parents who were rushing their daughter and putting her (and everyone else) in a very difficult and complicated situation to fulfill their own needs or to do what they felt was best for her. Moral of the story? In life, there are rules for a reason. There are expiration dates, due dates, RSVP dates, and cutoff dates for a reason. We need to abide by them—or as Robert Fulgham stated in his telling and eloquent poem: play fair. Life has rules.

Chapter 6

Parents as Partners

Parents and teachers alike all have the same goal—to have a successful and memorable year, most importantly for their children. How do we do that? Well, there are many different things to keep in mind. First and foremost, remember that you the parents and we the teachers are all on the same team. We are all here as advocates of the children and to help them develop into the best version of themselves they can possibly be.

It is imperative to establish a solid and trusting relationship with your children's teacher. You know your children better than anyone in the entire world and have been their primary caregivers for approximately five years, but it's time to "share the road." Teachers have studied for years to do what they do. They have taken classes and exams in psychology, statistics, classroom management, as well as the subject content area they are responsible for. And if you're really lucky, your child's teacher has all the qualities of a good teacher that can't be taught but are innate—acceptance, patience, and natural instinct. It is to the child's benefit to allow the teachers to do their job as hard as it may be sometimes to let go. The children you know at home may very well not be the same children the teachers know in the classroom. The classroom is *their* world—not the one you have created for them at home. You do not have full control any longer over who they play with all day or who they choose to spend their time with. You will not be there when they don't like the person they have to sit next to simply because your daughter thinks the boy is gross or your son thinks the girl is annoying. You will not be there when your timid child reads in class for the first time or has the courage to raise his hand. Your child will be on his own for Show and Tell and you won't be able to whisper in his ear all the things you told him to say. This is all okay!

But do not fret; you have given your children the tools they need to handle themselves in these situations. You are going to be fine and they are going to be even better—believe me. Hopefully your child will have a kindergarten teacher who looks at the children as his or her own. That can mean praising as well as reprimanding when necessary. We need to form a union that teaches the child that we are working together. Although parents know their child best, they don't necessarily know their child in the classroom.

I had a little girl in my class years ago who was the tiniest and smartest child I had ever seen. It came time for parent–teacher conferences and both parents attended. They were very serious people by nature but seemed especially concerned and nervous. I had only wonderful things to tell them about their daughter. She was polite, sweet, very hard working, and got along beautifully with her classmates. I showed them some of her work samples and expected them to be very pleased. Their daughter was also reading on a second-grade reading level—things were going very well. I thought we were about to conclude our conference when the mother hesitantly asked me about her behavior. I repeated that she got along just fine with the other children and was an excellent listener. The father finally had the courage to ask the looming question that was hanging over both of their heads: Was she biting anyone in class? I paused and tried to remain cool. I tried to look very official, as if I were referring to some very important and highly classified documents, so I double-checked my class list—*Do I have the right child here?* I wondered. *Have I been in this conference for fifteen minutes discussing the wrong child?* I mean—I didn't have any biters that I knew of in my class, but certainly one or two who seemed that *maybe* ... if provoked could get mildly physical, but not this little angel.

After quickly double-checking I confirmed that yes, this was the right child and the right parents. We continued our conversation. "I'm sorry—did you ask if she was *biting* in class?"

They both nodded yes. Parents across the globe, rest assured that if your child had bitten anyone in school, I'm confident you would have been notified by the school immediately! Biting is never okay and certainly never permitted. In fact, I'm not even sure your child would be allowed back in the classroom!

I could not believe my ears when they told me this was a huge problem at home, as well as her extreme explosive temper. They went on to tell me how she has fits of rage and could tear her room apart in record time. I was in complete shock. The description of this child was the polar opposite of the child I knew in school—I'm talking Jekyll and Hyde material. So while this example is without a doubt one of the more extreme cases (thank goodness), it is still an example of varying behavior between home and school.

A less extreme example but prevalent nonetheless is one of my own son. Let's just say that my youngest guy was born with a strong spirit—after all, his name actually means "man of fire" in Gaelic, so I'm not sure if this is a self-fulfilling prophecy or not. I can remember my husband and me bringing him to an open house at the school he would be attending for kindergarten. We were nervous wrecks to bring him as his behavior was somewhat unpredictable, for lack of a better word. I can remember the prospective principal asking him, "So are we going to see you in September?" and we jokingly replied, "Sure, if you'll have him!" This was a boy who for five years had smashed Corning Ware dishes for fun, ran through the entire house with the toilet paper roll (still attached to the wall in the bathroom), and pulled the dog by his tail on a regular basis—all for fun. My own mother called me every week in the beginning of pre-K to see if the teacher had called home yet. No one called, so I figured we were safe. I approached her a few weeks in just to be sure things were okay, and she told me that since I was inquiring ... he was a bit "eager." Eager? I never thought of that word with a negative connotation before, but her tone was a dead giveaway.

Hmmm ... "eager." I had to think about that one for a while. What was that really "code" for? What was she *really* saying to me? He finally got off to kindergarten and we never received one bad report. In fact, it was quite the opposite! Our son was doing just great in school, making lots of new friends and behaving as he should. So much of what we worry about are things that will work themselves out in time. So many of the behaviors we see at home and are worried that they may be carried out in the classroom are issues that deal with maturity. They are behaviors we cannot rush. Someone once used a funny expression: "street angels/house devils." I'll take it. I'd rather know my child is behaving properly and respectfully out of the home than in the home if I had to pick.

The reason children act out more at home than in school is simple. Home is where they feel safest. They are surrounded by the people who love them the most and unconditionally. This is why they will test the waters and push the boundaries—you are going to love them no matter what and they know this. While of course it would be a perfect world if all children behaved as they should at home and at school 100 percent of the time, it is not. I know I didn't and I'd bet you didn't either. If you don't believe me, ask your parents. Ask them to recall a few stories from your own childhood just to help you remember and relate to your child. This is all part of the unpredictable yet rewarding path of parenthood. Teaching is not much different; just when you've figured out how to handle one situation, a new one arises. It's a series of phases really, and it ebbs and flows like the tide. The beauty of it though is that we are all in it together.

I can recall a time when my daughter was in kindergarten and would forget something different every day. She would leave her lunch box, a homework sheet, a mitten—you name it—everyday in the classroom. It was getting frustrating and causing us anxiety. I thought it would be a brilliant idea to make a checklist for her and tape it to her little desk in school (she was able to read). So I made one up and went to visit the teacher to let her know I was here to solve one of life's major crises.

The teacher politely listened to me and my plan. She waited for me to stop and then patiently said, "Mrs. Podest, that won't be necessary. She'll get it eventually." What? Perhaps she wasn't hearing me properly. I had a solution, and a fantastic one at that! She explained that while I had an admirable idea, it really wasn't what my daughter needed. If the other students could get through packing up at the end of the day without a checklist, so could she. She just needed to listen better and pay attention to end-of-the-day instructions. She would eventually, in time, catch on. What the teacher was gently telling me was to stop holding my daughter's hand. She would figure it out on her own. She will continue to forget from time to time, but she would remember on her own soon enough. In other words, let her be responsible and take care of what she had to do—without Mommy's help. In the end, the teacher was absolutely right—who needs an embarrassing note in Mommy's handwriting anyway? Not my girl—yes, I was a little bit insulted, kicked in the gut just a bit. After all, no one had ever told me, much less disagreed with me, on what was best for my daughter. I then realized the teacher wasn't going against me, she was helping me go with her to play for the same team.

Another thing to consider when your child is starting school is to think about what your child is going to bring for a snack and/or lunch. This topic can be a real deal breaker when trying to make friends. You do not want your child to be known as the kid with the smelly sandwich now, do you? Of course not. Even if your child's favorite thing in the world is tuna or sushi, you might want to save those for meals at home. It may sound silly but it really is offensive if you are not used to those aromas and you're trying to enjoy a nice bologna sandwich. (By the way, I'm a huge fan of both tuna and sushi—I just know they both have their place.)

My daughter's kindergarten teacher had apparently made an announcement to the class that she did not want anyone bringing in little cups of peaches (you know, the ones with the clear, plastic tops on them that you peel back?). I had been sending them in several times a week as my daughter loved them and they were easy to pack. How dare she tell my daughter that! I didn't really believe the teacher had said this—maybe she just made a reference to the class that she wasn't a fan of them for some reason—who knows? But my daughter refused to bring these peaches and did not want me to say anything to her teacher about this either. I listened to my daughter but I was annoyed.

Years and years later when I had returned to the kindergarten classroom after a thirteen-year, baby-rearing hiatus, I not only remembered what the teacher had said about those peaches, but I agreed with her! When your child is eating in school (and most times, at the kindergarten level, it is done in the classroom), guess who helps the children open their snacks or lunch? That's right—the teacher. Day after day I wore peach juice on my blouse as it spurted out of the container, as did yogurt, applesauce, and many other yummy concoctions. While I was so tempted to make the same announcement to my class that my daughter's teacher had made years before, I tried something different. I actually gave them a lesson on how to open these things on their own. For some this entailed standing over the garbage can to prevent spillage and taking a nice big slurp of the peach juice before they too wore it. It sounds so menial, but I have a favor to ask you parents on behalf of teacher's everywhere. Take the time at home to show your child how to open a pretzel bag (even the bag shows you how!) or how to open a straw wrapper. Not only is this a big time saver for the teacher, it's usually a skill most kids can master. I have seen the pride on the faces of the independent child who not only opened his or her things alone but helped out a neighbor with his or her lunch box as well. If your child can't get it at first, he or she eventually will. In the meantime, the teacher is available to help.

Let's move on to signing papers and teacher correspondence. There are so many papers and forms that come home all year long and even more so in the beginning of the school year. Permission slips, book club orders, class picture forms, and school directories are just a few to mention. It is extremely helpful to the teacher if you fill these out, sign them, and return them in a timely manner. If there is an exact date required, you should respect that. If something comes home in the beginning of the week, try to get it back in by the end of the week. It is beneficial to establish a system at home in order to stay organized. It is imperative if you have more than one child in school—the paperwork can be overwhelming.

What many parents don't realize it that part of teaching is efficiently running a classroom. This portion of my job requires an administrative approach, and much of it is in conjunction with the main office. If forms come home from the school that require your attention, you need to realize there are countless other classrooms doing the same thing. It takes a lot of coordinating and time to get these things done accurately. Please be considerate of that fact. If you are not the type of person who is generally organized or punctual about responses, it is time to work on that. Your child is part of a big network now, and your teacher is the liaison between you and the main office. It can be helpful to have a special school calendar you have to write school-related notes on. It also helps to keep a separate folder or binder in which you can file away any pending papers that require your attention or notes you may want to keep for future reference. Keep these items in a safe place that is easy to retrieve. If the teacher has a "signed homework" policy, you need to follow it, and I will tell you why. It is my policy to have the parents sign their children's homework each night. This tells me the parent knows exactly what we are learning in school each day and that they have reviewed the lesson to some degree with their child. I know this can be a challenge for some parents who work (I work too so I understand this) but it's important. It's another form of communication between the parent and the teacher.

Your kindergarten teacher should be clear in establishing other procedures as well, including how birthdays are celebrated, dismissal procedures, going home with other parents on playdates, and more. If your child's teacher says goodies may be sent in to celebrate a birthday, find out what is acceptable. It is never a good idea to send in a cake that needs to be cut and served or worse – — one of those "cupcake breakaway cakes" (you know, the ones that look like a cake but are really twenty-four cupcakes underneath the icing?). I have actually had parents send in a camera, goodie bags, and a knife for cutting a cake—in short, I was hosting their child's birthday party. Remember that this is part of the actual school day and less is more—keep it simple and individualized such as a cupcake, a brownie, or a cookie. Remember to send in napkins or a plate as well to be served on.

Another topic that should be crystal clear from day one is the dismissal procedure. I am extremely strict about this and bend my rules for no one. It is not my intention to be difficult or to put anyone out, but I will in no way bend my dismissal policy for anyone. It is my responsibility to be 100 percent sure that I know who each child has gone home with for safety reasons and security purposes. I have been put in the position too many times where a parent forgets to call the office that a change in pickup has occurred. A friend or family member was sent and I was not notified. I have not, nor will I ever, release the child unless I've gotten the change in writing from the parent or received a call from the office.

Sadly, I have seen discord between parents going through custody battles that resulted in confusion at dismissal. This can be so upsetting for the child. I even had a mother send a friend I had never met before because the mom was in her car on the phone! I pray that no teacher would ever release my child to anyone other than the designated adult, and that is what I practice with my students. Send a note or call in advance—it's that simple. If you have enough time to call your friend to pick up your child, then you have had enough time to call the main office. Whatever your school's policy is on pick up and dismissal—respect it and abide by it. No exceptions. It is all devised with the safety and well-being of your child in mind. If an emergency arises at the last minute, call the school office. Most schools have a PA system and can get a last-minute message to the teacher that way. Please remember that the teacher's time is as valuable as yours and that it is your responsibility to be punctual. Don't delay in the schoolyard chatting with other parents. Receive your child first and then socialize. If it is difficult for you to get to school on time because you have younger children, perhaps a napping baby, make arrangements ahead of time. Maybe you can help one another out and share drop-off/pickup responsibilities a few times a week. Try to have a plan for picking up from school ahead of time. The school day has ended for the child but the teacher most likely still has hours of work ahead either in the classroom or what he or she brings home.

If you need to get in touch with your teacher regarding a question or concern, do so as soon as possible. It's best to address things from the beginning rather than let them linger or have too much time pass. You teacher should inform you at the beginning of the school year (certainly by back-to-school night) the best way to correspond. Some teachers prefer e-mail, some prefer scheduling a meeting, and for some a simple handwritten note will do. They should inform you of this and if for some reason they don't, be sure to ask. Remember that while your concern may seem imminent, the teacher is probably responding to you after school hours and may need a little time to get back to you. The teacher should let you know what his or her usual turnaround time is for a response. If your child's teacher is a member of your community, you need to respect the boundaries and realize this person has a life outside of school and very often has children as well. It is never okay to call the teacher at home (unless the teacher has given out his or her personal number and permission). School-related issues should be handled only at school and within school hours.

Chapter 7

Playdates and Extracurricular Activities

When my second-oldest child started kindergarten, she had already been taking dance class for three years. She loved it. Right before school began, I went to her dance studio to get the fall schedule and see how we were going to make this work now that she was in school full-time. In the past she had taken morning classes that coincided with her preschool schedule. But things were going to be different now and she would have to attend after school. No problem—her schedule was wide-open. We chose a Wednesday for no apparent reason and she would go from 4:00 to 5:00 p.m. I thought this would be perfect because it would give us enough time to go home after school, have a snack, do her little bit of homework, and get changed.

To my surprise it did not work our exactly like that. Most days when we got home my daughter would have her snack and then disappear. At first I thought she was just trying to get out of doing her homework before dance class, but this was not the case. She had gone into her room and fallen asleep on her bed! The next time I found her on the couch curled up with our dog, dreaming away. I was so shocked by this as she wasn't really one to nap and really hadn't unless she was sick. She was also one of the oldest in the class and always so mature. However, this new full-day schedule seemed to be all she could handle at this point. I gave it three weeks and decided to call the studio to see what we could do. They let me put her dance class off to a later date when she might be a bit more acclimated to her new routine. This worked out for the best because she also joined Girl Scouts through school (which worked out fine because it was at school and immediately after school, leaving little to no time for her to get too sleepy) and played soccer in our town on Saturday mornings. Throw in a few playdates with some new friends and you've got yourself one busy little girl!

So here's what I'm telling you—you need to realize that life as you once knew it is different now. The schedule is not the same, and really, neither is your child. Your child is growing and learning and may start to express interest in trying new activities or playing with new friends. This is all wonderful and part of the kindergarten process. I think it's important to listen to your child at this time. Every child is so different, and really, you the parent knows him or her best. It is your job to guide and steer your child in the right direction but allow him or her some input. Have you ever seen the child at practice or at a dance class who really didn't want to be there? He or she was either too shy or just had no interest. You know the one—the parent usually has to bribe him or her with a doughnut or a hot chocolate when the child gets off the field—if he or she agrees to go in the first place. I've seen it over and over, and I think it's a mistake to force the child.

You know your children—early on we expose them to different sports, activities, etc. and see what they like best. They may not love everything they try. Our goal was always to let them try something and if they didn't like it, the deal was they had to finish the season out and we would rethink the whole thing before signing up the next year. That was the case with our youngest child. His three older siblings had all played soccer for years. One of them went on to play for a travel team in the spring and fall for seven years. But when our little guy got out on that soccer field, all he cared about was socializing. It didn't matter which team you were on either—he just wanted to talk and make friends. He would be running up and down the field during the game asking whoever was closest to him, "Are you hungry? I'm starving!" We would be on the sidelines yelling, "Stop talking and pay attention!" Clearly this wasn't working, and truthfully, it was kind of funny to watch. No matter what we said to him, it didn't matter—he was thrilled he was making new friends (and enjoying the team snack at the end of the game)! He really had no interest in the game. Needless to say, it was a short-lived soccer career but that was okay. He was on to bigger and better things.

Give new things a try, whether it's through your school, your town, or other organizations and see what they like. Remember that all children are different and younger siblings may not follow the footsteps of the older siblings. You also need to consider what works for your family and your family's schedule. If you are a working parent, you may want to consider carpooling. You may have a new baby at home that you don't want to take out into the cold or into a loud and germ-filled gymnasium. This is a good time to make connections with the parents and families around you. We all need to lean on each other from time to time and to help lighten each other's load just a bit. Do not feel for one second that you are not a good parent or that your child will be scarred if you are not watching through the glass or on the sidelines of every practice. Truthfully, most coaches and/or teachers would prefer that you leave anyway. It's much easier to coach and teach children if they know their parents are not there watching. This is their time, in their own little world. Don't be afraid to give them this space and this little bit of freedom. This is how they grow. You've given them everything they need at this point, so trust yourself and them that they will be okay—they will survive on their own for an hour. You've already taught them what they need to know.

This brings me to the topic of playdates. I still struggle with the actual term, playdates. To me, it's an oxymoron. You have to make a date to play. That's not how it worked when I was growing up, and I'm going to guess it was different for you as well. My mother almost never drove me to play at someone's house, and I know for sure she didn't take out a calendar to see when I was free. It really is a crazy world we live in. Everything is planned out in advance and scheduled. Sports practices and games schedules take precedence over family time and very often religious worship. We are living like hamsters on the wheel and we just can't get off. The days of ringing someone's doorbell are more of a distant memory. If you are fortunate enough to live in a neighborhood or a community where you have neighbors with children who are available to play with your children, you are one of the lucky ones. I'm referring here more so to children in the suburbs of the United States whose neighborhoods are spread farther apart, and most have two working parents who are probably commuting a distance from home and may not even have time to get to know their neighbors.

When I was growing up, you knew every single family on the block. And most families had lots of kids. We were the smallest family on the block with three girls. Our neighbors had anywhere from four to twelve kids each! That makes for one lively and outrageous Halloween—ghosts, witches, and goblins abound! When we were outside, you played with kids of all ages and half the time my mother didn't even know exactly where we were. I was outside playing. Just be home in time for supper; that was the rule. My mother was in no way cavalier or remiss—it was just a different time, a different world. We had all the freedom we wanted.

When my husband and I reminisce about those days, our children hang on every word and ask a hundred questions. Was Nana worried? You were allowed to ride your bike *how* far from home? One of my favorite memories was how we would all come back outside after dinner and even our bath in the summertime. We would get one last game of kickball going (in our baby-doll pajamas with pink sponge rollers in our hair) before hitting the hay. It was a much more carefree and simpler way of life. I long for those days and have tried my hardest to somehow, to the best of my ability, give my own children some of the freedoms we enjoyed when we were growing up.

Sadly we all know it's not like that so much anymore. Parents are much more hesitant to allow their children to go on playdates and even more so if it's someone they just met—and rightfully so. I'm a parent too and I share those concerns. Is there a pool in the yard? Do they have guns in the house? Do they have older children in the home? Will the mother or the father be supervising? So many questions and concerns that we torture ourselves with. It's almost impossible not to if you read the paper or watch the news.

So how do we allow our children to establish friendships and relationships with new classmates? These very well may be families you have never met before and have no mutual friend to do an informal background check with. What I have found in the past is that it is your responsibility as a parent to get to know some of the parents in your child's class. You don't need to meet every single one or become best friends with everyone, but it will be to your child's benefit if you have a few contacts and people know who you are. Of course this is more of a challenge for the working parents (another oxymoron—don't all parents "work"?

Of course we do!) or parents who travel in their careers. It is also difficult for children who come from divorced families and live between two different residences. But it can be done—I've seen it. In fact, these parents may need to meet other parents more than anyone. This way you have a contact in the class in case you have a question or are able to help each other out. As I stated previously, you may want to try to save a day off, take a half day, or work from home on the first day of school. Try to be at pickup a few minutes earlier so you have the opportunity to talk with other parents—introduce yourself to one or two other parents. You might even notice a grandparent or a stay-at-home dad who may be the one in the schoolyard each day—try to reach out if you can. They may be a little nervous or uncomfortable as well and looking for someone to connect with. Realistically speaking, it is more common and probably more natural to see a group of moms (a.k.a. women) chatting it up together than the seventy-five-year-old grandmother or the father who is home raising his family. It's so much easier and truthfully just plain nicer for everyone when you see a familiar face at school—someone to smile at you, say hi, and share the school year experience with.

One way of getting to meet some families in your school is to organize a group playdate at a local park so no one has to host and several kids can come. This way all the parents can socialize and everyone is responsible for their own children. You might get a sense in that setting who you connect with as well as who your child is having fun with. This is a good time to exchange cell numbers with another parent or two. Perhaps you would feel comfortable trying a playdate at one of your homes next time. Children bond so quickly over showing a classmate their family dog or sharing their favorite toys. It is through this interaction that children develop relationships with each other that they can easily carry into the classroom. This lends itself to a sense of belonging, establishing friendships, and a comfort level that enables them to be themselves in the classroom.

Another place to meet up with a friend from school is your local library. The children's section is usually a place you don't have to be silent. Very often librarians even promote and encourage talking! This is the perfect situation to get together for a while and have some fun—free of charge, no less! When my sisters and I were growing up, our mom took us to the library in our town once a week. I couldn't wait to go and see what new books were available for me to check out! We also enjoyed participating in story time and very often stayed for a snack or a craft. This still goes on in libraries nationwide and is a service that surprisingly many parents are unaware of. Each year, I send a note home to my students' parents informing them about how the US library system works. In many towns, all children age five and older are eligible to get their very own library card. My children always thought this was the best thing in the world! They thought it was a credit card for books and couldn't believe everything was free. Many cities and towns also take part in an integrated book system, where you can use your library card in any of the libraries within your county. This means you can check books out from a library in a neighboring town and can return the books to any library or book drop within that county. Brilliant, right? I think so and want as many parents as possible to know about this. I know we live in a world of Kindles and Nooks, but there is nothing like curling up with a good book and actually turning a page to see what happens next. It's even better when shared with a friend—bring your kindergartner soon, and don't forget to let your child get his or her own card. Soon enough, your child will be begging you to go.

Chapter 8

Back-to-School Night and Getting Involved

At the beginning of every school year, the school will host a back-to-school night. This is usually done in September and is the perfect way to get an overview of the school year. The evening usually starts with a general assembly in which the principal or other heads of committees may speak for a few minutes and then direct you where to go from there. Once you are in your child's classroom, you will have the opportunity to see where he or she sits, how the classroom is set up, and how your child's work will be displayed.

It has been my experience that the students are usually very excited to know that their mom or dad will be visiting their classroom that night. You may get to sit in their chair or at their desk and see their perspective of the classroom. They may have left you a special picture. You may have the opportunity to look through their journal or see what they are working on. I always think it is nice to leave a special surprise as well. If your child is already a fairly fluent reader, by all means, leave a note. If your child is not yet reading (it is only September of kindergarten, so don't panic! Most children are not yet reading) leave a Hershey's

Kiss with a smiley face or a "Love Mom or Dad" note. Draw a heart—something that will be clear that they know you were there and you love them. It's a simple little gesture that speaks volumes to your little ones—the smiles on their faces are priceless when they come into school the next day.

Usually the teacher will address the parents and go over the general curriculum and other "housekeeping" details you may need to know. He or she will probably ask if there are any questions. If you have a question about something the teacher may have said or anything else you want to know regarding the school year, this is a good time to ask. This is not the time for a personal conference or to speak specifically about your child. That being said, do not be afraid to ask something you are unsure of or would like clarified. Chances are someone else in the room is wondering the same thing. Try to make a point to say good-bye and thank you to the teacher before you leave. It is somewhat overwhelming for the teacher at this point trying to remember who is who and which parent belongs to which child. A simple good-bye, eye contact, and a handshake are the things that have helped me in the past remember who I was speaking with.

This is the very beginning of establishing a relationship with your child's teacher. You've just met your new "teammate" for the school year! If for some reason you are unable to attend back-to-school night (maybe you're traveling, maybe you have a new baby at home and can't get out—although, sadly, when I had a new baby and was looking for any excuse to get out of the house, this was a big and exciting night for me! Maybe you are stuck at work, couldn't get a babysitter—whatever the case may be), try to contact the teacher ahead of time. Otherwise, reach out to the teacher as soon as possible. This way the teacher can send home any handouts or important papers that may be distributed that evening.

You might also request the names of the "class parents" if your school does that. Very often, two or so parents are asked to be the class parents for the year. They are a liaison between the parents and the teacher and may assist the class in different ways that the teacher and the school see fit. It is good to have those contacts in case you have any questions throughout the school year.

Kindergarten is a very unique year, and one of the things that I have always loved about it is that we celebrate all of life's little special moments. We celebrate the Student of the Week, a lost tooth, great behavior, and of course birthdays and every single holiday we can think of. We have a big Thanksgiving feast and celebrate the 100th Day of Kindergarten. This is also the year where Girl Scouts or Boy Scouts may begin for your child. I can't say enough about how much the children love to be part of scouts. The problem seems to be in many towns that the children are in need of a leader. I became my son's Tiger Scout leader when he was young, and I shared the role with two other mothers. I had just given birth to my third child and I really didn't think I could commit to this. The three of us divided the responsibilities and made it work. The boys had a blast, and truthfully, I enjoyed myself as well. Who knew that "getting out of the house" would mean getting a babysitter to go spend time with fifteen scouts—man, how my life had changed! Organizing scouts may become part of the responsibility of the class parent to help organize and plan for the year. If this is the case, be sure you offer or volunteer something at some point through the year. The children take immense pride in telling their peers that *my* mom made these cupcakes or *my* dad picked out these awesome plates for the Valentine's Day party. It also fosters a sense of community when we all pitch in and come together. These years are going to fly by so much quicker than you can even imagine. You don't want to look back and regret that you didn't make it more special because you didn't want to get involved. Everyone is busy. So if we all take on a little bit of the responsibilities, no one will be inundated with a big job. Many hands lighten the load!

Another thing to consider now that you are part of the school community is how to volunteer and show support for your child's kindergarten class. I know what some of you are thinking— another thing on my to-do list? There is barely enough time to do what we *have* to do, never mind what we *should* do, and you can just forget what we *want* to do—that's on the bottom of the totem pole of life. But getting involved does not have to be an all-consuming role or a part-time job. There really is something for everyone to do. There are certain parents who live for helping out in school whenever and however they can. Some people have more time than others, and God bless them for making themselves available. None of us can do this alone or make the school the environment and community what we want it to be—alone. We are all in this together. What benefits my child will in the long run benefit your child.

Every school is different and has different policies regarding volunteering. Some schools do not require or mandate any volunteer time from the parents while some schools have a specific guideline of what they need from each family. Find out your school's policy and see what works for you. If you are absolutely unable to attend any school function where volunteers are needed because of outside responsibilities or time restrictions, don't feel bad. Maybe you can make phone calls for a certain committee at a time that works for you, perhaps you are computer savvy and are able to type up the minutes to a meeting that went on, or you can print labels for an upcoming school mailing. Maybe you can bake something and send it in, or if that's too much, there's a great aisle in every grocery store with goodies galore to choose from (shh … I won't tell if you don't!). Just do what you can when you can. That's really all any of us can ever do. Also, always assume everyone is doing the very best they can at all times. I truly feel most of us are.

Chapter 9

Conferences, Report Cards, and Communication

From time to time, a teacher may send a note home or place a phone call if he or she has a concern to share or a problem has arisen in the classroom. I believe this is the sign of a teacher who cares. As difficult as it may be, try not to become defensive or take it personally. Very often, when I send a note home regarding a concern that I may have about a child, the parent immediately takes it as an attack on his or her parenting skills. Remember, this is not about you. This is about your child and the life he or she leads in school. I have found this to be especially true for new parents who have their first child in kindergarten (and remember—I was one of you also at one point).

"What do you mean he is not listening?" "What do you mean she is not following directions?" "My son would never push on the playground unless he was provoked!"

Slow down, moms and dads! This is not a battle. It is merely an attempt for your child's teacher to keep the lines of communication open between all the caring adults in the child's life. It is best, at this time, to have a conversation on the phone or in person at a time that is convenient for both of you. Parents who become defensive are also emotional, and parents who are emotional can say things they don't mean.

For example, I had a little girl in my class once who was just completely out of it on one particular Friday morning. She couldn't keep her head up, couldn't participate in any of the class activities, and couldn't complete her work. I felt her head and she was not warm but her eyes were glazed over and she was clearly not well. So I sent her to the school nurse to see if she could figure out what was going on with this little girl. Now let me preface this with the fact that it was the end of the week, and the child was in school from 8:00 a.m. until 6:00 p.m. because she also attended the after-school program daily. She said she was up a lot during the night and that she was just "really, really tired." I was exhausted just thinking about this little girl's schedule!

Being extremely tired is something we have all experienced at one time or another—maybe we were unable to drive because we were so tired or we canceled plans at the last minute because we just couldn't move at the end of the day or by the end of the week. If you've ever been up all night with a newborn, you know the type of tired I am talking about—true exhaustion is real. It is real to adults and it sure is real to five-year-old children. If your child is *so* exhausted that he or she cannot function in school, the child needs to go home. The child may not be physically sick per se, but he or she is not well either.

Now I know this is not always convenient, especially for the working parents. But guess what? It is *your* responsibility to have a backup plan, a tried and true plan B. Of course we all have to fill out those emergency cards at the beginning of the school year, but you need to have someone you can rely on to help you out in an emergency. If you don't have family nearby, make arrangements with a neighbor or a stay-at-home parent that you know and be prepared to pay someone, as I have, had to do. Whatever you have to do to be able to pick up your child from school or have someone else do it—then do it. Be prepared.

So let's get back to my student in the nurse's office. When the nurse called the mother to say her daughter was not well, the mother was very annoyed and questioned the nurse. If she didn't have a fever, then why did she have to come get her? The nurse explained further and the mother angrily hung up, saying she would be there when she could. The mother retrieved her child and within thirty minutes had e-mailed me and the school principal to request a meeting with her and her husband to discuss the "incident."

What? Excuse me? What "incident" was she talking about? I was under the impression that something else had happened that I was unaware of when the word "incident" was used. Nope—the "incident" was that her daughter was sent to the nurse's office and sent home from school. I was speechless. Never in all my years had a parent ever questioned my motive for sending an unwell child to the nurse. In fact, if anything, I've been guilty of holding on to the nurse's office "frequent fliers" too long and have had some projectile vomiters in my classroom!

Well, we had a meeting the following week, and it was one of the more interesting meetings I've ever had. Both parents wanted to know if their child had been sent to the nurse's office for bad behavior or not doing her work. *What? Am I hearing this correctly?* They wanted to impress upon me, as they had impressed on their five-year-old, that they both worked and that they explained to their daughter that it was *her* job to stay in school. This little girl had never even been to the nurse's office before and she went because I had sent her—not because she asked to go! I was trying very hard to remain professional, but my blood was boiling.

I explained to them that as a parent, I would appreciate a call from the school if my child was not feeling well, and I would be more concerned if the child was coming down with something. It is not the school's intention to jeopardize the parents' entire day, but remember—you *are* the parent and are responsible for your child's health and well-being. Sadly, the parents had made it clear to the little girl that she was not allowed to go to the nurses' office ever again (I kid you not) or they would be really mad at her.

Two days later during recess, the little girl had an accident in her pants. She did not get to the bathroom in time and did not want to tell the lunch monitor that she had a bowel movement because her parents told her that she was not allowed to go to the nurses' office anymore. This poor baby would rather stay in her own feces than get cleaned up because she knew she was going to be in big trouble with Mommy and Daddy.

When the mother was called again, she was annoyed and said she would be there when she could. That was one hour later. For one hour that poor child stood in her own filth. For the life of me I will never understand some people. It is not my job to teach them or tell them how to raise their child, but every once in a while, I sure wish I could.

It could be something somewhat serious (getting physical with another student, taking someone's things, bad language in school), or it could be something minor (being unkind to a classmate, constant talking, not being able to stay in their seat, etc.) that the teacher just wants to bring to your attention. Occasionally, a teacher may need to speak to you about something that happened between your child and another child and although it was nothing earth shattering, the teacher is giving you a heads-up. No matter what the situation is, do not panic. More importantly, don't get your back up and be defensive, and don't punish your child before you get the facts!

Let's say you want to set up a meeting with your child's teacher just to check in. Or perhaps you have a question or concern you would like to address. How do you go about this properly? Personally, I appreciate a note or an e-mail. Keep it brief and state the fact that you would like to meet and ask when might be a good time.

Now ... here's the kicker. Working parents often make requests that very simply may not work for the teacher. "Before work hours" really means before *your* work hours because guess what? The teacher is already at work! I understand that parents have trains to catch and deadlines to meet, really I do. But what is often forgotten is that not only do I have a job to do as well, my job is with your child! If you request a meeting at any time other than conference time, you need to be flexible and work around the teacher's schedule as well. I know I do everything I can to accommodate the parents—after all, we're all in this together and want the same positive end result. So try to remember to be flexible and realize you may very well have to adjust your workday—because the teacher has just adjusted his or hers in order to meet with you.

When it comes to official parent–teacher conferences, kindergarten is different from other grades in that some of the things the children are being evaluated on are concrete and tangible, such as math tests and reading assessments, while other things such as behavior, emotional growth, and personal development cannot be measured numerically. Your school may or may not have a report card system of sorts. More often than not there is some formal, written communication sent home throughout the year from the teacher to the parents. It may be done two, three, or four times a year as new concepts are introduced and the child is maturing.

Children in kindergarten are at such a crucial time in their lives. They are crossing an invisible bridge from one part of their lives to the next. They have so much to learn this year, and so much of it will not come from a book. As parents, we have navigated their every move and guided every decision up to this point. But now they are on their own. Of course I am there for them as their teacher and surrogate parent, but it is time for them to start thinking for themselves in a way they have never had to before. They are deciding who they will play with, who they will share a book with, which part of their lunch or snack they eat first (warning! Cookies may come before apple slices at this time—sorry!); they will be responsible when using the bathroom, cleaning up after themselves, taking turns, raising their hands, forgiving someone who has wronged them, being a good listener, using manners—oh, and did I mention reading, writing, phonics, math, and more? It's a great big umbrella that we stand under in kindergarten, and it is amazing for me to see these children unfold all year long to become the young people of tomorrow. I cherish every moment of it, and this is exactly what I want to share with you at conference time.

Conferences are a special and important time for parents and teachers to come together, reacquaint themselves, and listen to one another. I love conference time. Do you need to attend if there is absolutely no issue at hand and you have received a stellar and glowing report card? Yes—please make every effort to attend. Not only is it a great time to connect with the teacher and check in with the school, but your child wants you to go. Studies show that children are more successful in school when their parents express interest. Conference time allows for this. It is a time for me to talk to the parents, and mostly I love to listen. The one thing I have learned without fail is that the children who live in your house are not the exact same children who live in my classroom. How could they be? They don't have their family in school with them, they don't have the comfort of their bedroom to play quietly or retreat to if a problem arises, they can't really (or at least shouldn't) melt down when things don't work out, they don't have their favorite stuffed animal or doll, and they can't grab a snack whenever they feel like it or lay down if they want to! No, life in school is very different, and there are different rules. Rules, procedures, routines, consequences—and worse ... maybe some kids they don't even like! How are they getting through the day? Usually just fine for the most part. And that is what the teacher is looking to share with you. If there is some serious problem that is going on in school that needs attention, this should have been previously addressed. Parents should never come to a parent–teacher conference and get some sort of big surprise about their child's behavior or academic progress.

I like to start out the conference asking the parents if they have any concerns or questions. Usually the conference tone is set from there. I learn so much about each child every time I speak with a parent. Families are an interesting, diverse, and very funny unit. I can often see how the class clown in my class came to be if the parent is especially humorous, or the gentle, shy child whose parent is particularly soft-spoken and low-key. I can now understand why the "overachiever" is so hard on himself or herself because the parent has very high expectations. None of this is judgment—only observation.

I have had several encounters where I can sense a disconnect between the parents from the moment we sit down. Sometimes spouses don't always agree on parenting issues or don't share a concern they may have about their child. Occasionally the parents are not a couple anymore. If this is going to be uncomfortable for them to come together or become a "tension convention" with the teacher caught in the middle, then make separate appointments. I do not appreciate when a mother and father come to see me and you can cut the tension with a knife as soon as they walk in. I'm not your marital counselor or your referee. I am your child's teacher. Any issues between the two of you should be left outside the door. If you can't manage that, then you need to come separately. It is always best to iron this out at home before you come to your conference and focus on the important matter at hand—your child. Parents and teachers are in a vital partnership. Together they are at the helm of the student's happiness and success and must work as a team.

When you are meeting with the teacher, it is helpful to come prepared. Write down questions. If you have questions about work samples, bring them. Ask the teacher if he or she has any of your child's work that you may have not seen, like a journal or a copybook. Unfortunately, a parent–teacher conference is not an unlimited amount of time for either of you, and you should try to use your time as efficiently and wisely as possible.

Remember that at this age, you should be discussing every aspect of the child's growth and development, not just academics. Here are a few questions you may want to consider:

1) Does my child seem happy in school?
2) Is my child engaging and interacting with the other children?
3) Can you tell me one or two names of children he or she seems to enjoy spending time with?
4) Is my child listening and following directions?
5) Do you feel my child is progressing in an acceptable manner?
6) Is there anything you would like me to do with my child at home?
7) Is my child completing their work in a timely manner?
8) Are they respectful toward adults and other children?
9) Can you recommend any particular authors my child might enjoy who would be appropriate for their reading level?
10) Is there any area of growth that you are concerned with?

As I have said before, any major problems or concerns should not be addressed for the first time at a parent–teacher conference. You should have been contacted beforehand if it were serious or a major concern. It is important for you to remember when you go to a conference that other parents are waiting to see the teacher as well. You do not want to be known as the parent who monopolized the teacher's time (and *yes,* people will talk about you if you leave them out in the hall waiting for half an hour!). If you are unable to attend the conference, you should make other arrangements to meet your child's teacher to see how your child is doing. I have had parents who never showed up or contacted me to get together at another time and I was always disappointed. I even sent home notes to say, "You were missed!" to no avail. I enjoy and need to meet with the parents as much as they need to meet with me. Not only does it show interest to the teacher but it lets your children know how much you value them and their progress. What child doesn't love to hear from his or her parents, "I met with your teacher, and we are both so proud of you! You are doing such a beautiful job in school and working so hard!"

Please make every effort to attend or make other arrangements if necessary. Very often, a phone conference can be just as effective as a face-to-face meeting and might even be easier for working parents or parents who are home with small children.

Another point worth mentioning is that there are so many wonderful, positive, and exciting things your child's teacher wants to share with you, so make sure that at some point the two of you connect. To be honest, I get more excited and look forward to the meetings when I can tell parents about a small step or great strides their child has made. It gives us all hope and enthusiasm about that student's future—who doesn't love that? So often we question ourselves or doubt the decisions we have made regarding our children. The truth is we don't know for sure if we are doing exactly the right thing—all we can do is try our best and support one another. You are all wonderful, caring parents or you wouldn't be reading a book such as this one! Remember also that when you screw up—and you will—forgive yourself. You'll do better next time.

Occasionally I have a student who seems to be having some trouble adjusting to kindergarten. I try to give it until October before I address this with the parents because I feel this is a fair amount of time to allow the child to settle in to the new routine and procedures. At this point, he or she has made some new friends and gotten to know me better as well. Sadly though, I have had students I can immediately see have more serious issues that need to be addressed. Whether it be attention disorders, developmental or maturity-level issues, or something more serious, where evaluation and testing may be required, I don't like to waste too much time and will contact the parents sooner rather than later. This is always done in accordance with the school administration, which should be present at a requested meeting by the teacher. It is at this time that you, the parent, needs to honest and forthcoming with any information or prior evaluations that may be pertinent to the teacher's concern. It is a mistake to think that maybe, if the child has more time, he or she will grow out of whatever the problem may be. If there is an issue, problem, or concern that requires evaluation and testing so that the appropriate team of people may assist your child to further grow and develop, do not waste time. A process like this takes months to complete before a diagnosis can be made and an individual educational plan devised that best suits your child.

Years ago I had a little boy in my class who clearly had some developmental issues. I am not a special education teacher, nor do I claim to have an extensive background in this field. However, it did not take an expert to see that something needed to addressed.

I requested a meeting with the parents to explain what I had been seeing in the classroom, and I wanted to know a little bit more about this boy and his previous school experience. Had his previous teacher ever spoken to them about certain behaviors or concerns? According to the parents, no, never, not one time did any teacher, doctor, or professional mention one thing that seemed to be a red flag that this boy *possibly* required some further attention and assistance. I started to wonder if it was just me. Was I jumping the gun here? Maybe I was overreacting. The parents thanked me for my time and we agreed to be in contact if there were any further concerns.

The following week the boy began acting out more than he ever had before. He became verbally aggressive with classmates. He didn't make eye contact when he spoke to you. He repeatedly lined up chairs in a systematic fashion to simulate riding a bus and constantly stacked his crayons over and over again in the same Lincoln Log–style of building a cabin. He would completely melt down at lunchtime if his food wasn't the temperature he desired and would lay on the rug making pretend snow angels in an attempt to comfort himself.

Time for meeting number two. This time the mother came by herself. Again—nothing shared, nothing new learned here. This went on for two more weeks, and I approached the principal and requested he be present at a third meeting. This time we insisted that both parents attend.

This meeting was entirely different. Not only did the father show up in his medical scrubs (he was a surgeon) the mother finally produced previous evaluations and findings that had been concluded the previous year. How could a father with a medical background and obvious access to a host of support and pediatric doctors withhold such pertinent information? How could a mother sit through three meetings with a teacher and administration and waste our time as we scratched our heads trying to figure out what was really going on here? How could they dishonestly tell us no one had ever brought their son's behavior to their attention? Denial. Fear. Failure. Love. Until I have walked in those parents' shoes, I will not judge. I certainly disagree with the way they behaved and handled this situation, but it was not with malice or ill intent.

It is not always easy to see in our own children what others may see. Some parents see a problem as a reflection of themselves, but this is not true. Once the parents let the wall come tumbling down, we were able to help this boy and move forward. They began to trust us and knew that further testing was in his best interest. We were going to get him the appropriate services that he needed in the setting that was best for him.

I lost a lot of sleep over that little boy—I worried about him and what his life would be like if he didn't get the help he needed. In the end, the parents were able to see that we were partners and together we would work this out. I had not seen the boy or his family for years, and I recently ran into the father. I was so happy to hear that he was doing well and thriving in school. I always feared that the parents secretly resented my persistence, but on this day the father thanked me for my efforts. My fears were laid to rest.

Chapter 10

When There Are Problems at Home

I think many adults would be surprised if they realized how verbal their children can be in school regarding problems or situations at home. I'm actually grateful for this because it lets me know what is on their mind or what they may be feeling. Year after year I have seen children deal with some very heavy-duty stuff, stuff that adults struggle with and try to make sense of: terminal illness, death of a grandparent, loss of a pet, alcoholism, addictions, mental illness, separation, and divorce, and probably the worst—the death of a parent. Children are so extremely receptive and in tune with the vibe and energy in their home. Even if they are not part of the adult conversations that are going on, they feel the shift in the environment, whether it be tension, fear, sadness, or anger. These things can easily create confusion and anxiety for the child, and sometimes the safest way to express that is in school—with their teacher.

In my classroom, I have a little table and chair set up in a quiet corner. I leave a basket with a pencil and paper there for the children. They may write or draw a special intension on the paper, fold it up, put it in the basket, and say a prayer or just take a reflective moment. It is so amazing to see their sensitivity and pure thoughtfulness as they sit there and think about what they are writing. I purposely keep this table and chair near my desk so that I am aware of who is taking the opportunity to visit. This opens up the conversation between me and the child so that I may be of some help if they would like to discuss their feelings.

Kindergarten children feel so many of the exact same feelings adults feel. Sometimes they just don't understand or know how to articulate what is on their mind. Sadly, many children are exposed to the real world sooner than we had planned on, and they need a way to make sense of what is going on at home. I try to listen to them and comfort them when they need it. Some children are not as verbal about what they are going through, and it can be more difficult to know how to help. I try to follow their lead, read their body language, observe their interactions, and listen as they converse among themselves in an attempt to give them whatever it is they need.

If there is a serious situation that is going on at home or in the family, do your child a favor and fill the teacher in as best you can. I don't want to know anyone's personal business; I really don't. But it is foolish to think that because your children have walked out the front door to go to school they have left their feelings and concerns there too. Children can easily become withdrawn, act quieter than usual, and behave in an aggressive manner verbally or physically if there is something they are upset about. Your children's teacher can be a major support system for them and an ally to the parents as well. Very often children spend more time with their teacher than they do with their parents—let the teacher help. Informing the teacher of any change at home or situation that has arisen can only help your child to cope better.

It is often difficult to share personal information, especially if it has to do with you, the parent. But you need to remember what is best for your child, and keeping the teacher in the loop is what's best for your child. It has been my experience that a child will generally mirror their parents' behavior in dealing with a crisis or a tough situation. Let's consider a divided household—Mom lives in one home and Dad lives in another. If there is serious tension between the two adults, and let's be honest, there very often is, the child will be tense. If there is mutual respect and peace between the two adults, then the child will be more relaxed. If you are bitter and angry toward each other, that will be all your child knows—and that's not what you want, I'm sure. One of the hardest things in the world to do is to be amicable toward someone who has hurt you, but there isn't too much we wouldn't do for our children, right? If it is impossible to be cordial, then to your best ability, just fake it. There's no need to put an old head on little shoulders by burdening them with adult problems. They have their whole lives to learn about the real world.

I knew another student who was going through some kind of family trouble at home, but I wasn't sure what it was. The mom had approached me once to say that if her son was acting out or seemed a little off, it was probably a result of their family issues. She didn't really expand except to say that she and her husband were going through a hard time. The mom sort of disappeared after that, with different people picking her son up from school on a regular basis. Soon after, the grandmother became more of the primary caregiver. No one told me where the mother went, and I wasn't getting any information from the grandmother. I just wanted to able to help the boy in my class. It turned out that the mother was away for a few months getting help for addictions and mental issues that she needed to deal with. I applauded the mother for being so brave and for doing what she had to do. It could not be easy for any parent to be away from his or her child for an extended period of time, and God knows the child would be better off with a healthy and happy mother. However, for the life of me I will never understand how someone didn't think the boy's teacher should be made aware that his *mother* was gone. Can you imagine what was going through his head at this confusing time? It pains me to think of how deeply he missed her and how he seemed to keep that all inside. I wish I had been informed so that I could have helped more.

Parents, no one likes to air their dirty laundry. No one wants the world to know about our faults, problems, or imperfections. However, we need to see beyond ourselves and do what is in our child's best interest. Share, if you can, and to the best of your ability, when something serious is going on at home. It affects your child's well-being in every possible way. Let your teacher be a source of comfort and support when you can't be. There is no shame in honesty, because honestly? You are doing what is best for your child.

Chapter 11

You Can't Make This Stuff Up

Anyone who knows me will tell you that I have a pretty good sense of humor (and it sometimes gets me into a little bit of trouble, but that's okay!). I somehow see the hilarious in the ridiculous and the giggles in the grind of everyday life. My husband will say to me in certain situations, "I don't even want to know what's going through that head of yours right now!" as he knows my view of the world is just a little bit comically skewed.

It is with this mind-set that I approach my interaction with five and six year old people. Their pure innocence and perfect view of the world is something that is so far beyond our affected and sometimes jaded mentality. I absolutely relish my conversations and interactions with these perfect little beings. It is virtually impossible for a child of this age to be truly mean or manipulative. Children will believe almost anything you tell them and will trust and love you until the end of the earth. What other age group will undoubtedly believe that a two-inch fairy will fly into their rooms at night, take their sugar-covered little tooth, *and* pay them for it! It's beautiful and amazing.

I have had more fun and true belly laughs while teaching in my classroom over the years. Here are just a few of the great giggles that stand out.

The Only Stupid Question Is the One That Goes Unasked
It was the first day of school and we just went over a few simple rules and procedures. I asked the class, "Does anyone have any questions?" One boy raised his hand and with utter confusion on his face looked around the class and asked, "Um, excuse me? Where's the gift shop anyway?"

It's Always Sunny in Kindergarten
It was morning calendar time and we were going over the forecast for the day. As if on cue, an unexpected spring shower began and the quietest boy in my class raised his hand and uttered, "The weatherman is a big liar. He said it was going to be mostly sunny today."

Getting to Know You
It was the third week of my new teaching position in a very culturally diverse school district. My line leader was a boy's family who had just arrived in the states. His father was an opera singer and working at the Met in Lincoln Center in New York City. He was learning English and was quite shy but had a great big smile and warm demeanor. I thought making him line leader was the right thing to do so that he felt important and included. That is until the day he looked at me and took it upon himself to put both hands where they shouldn't go and gave me an unexpected squeeze! Not only did this boy catch me completely off guard, I was mortified! What should I do? I had to report this to someone—but who? My principal was a man my father's age, and it would be so awkward and embarrassing, but this couldn't be ignored. I did speak to my principal, and he told me it had to be addressed with the parents—further embarrassment! In doing

so, the mother was beyond horrified at her son's behavior and the father tried to hide his amusement as he apologized and told me his boy was just like Daddy! Too much information, Daddy. He later apologized with two tickets to see *La Traviata*. Not really a traditional apology, but we went and saw our first and only opera.

They *Will* Show and Tell

Show and Tell is big in kindergarten, and in my class we go by the letter of the week. This particular week, the letter was X/x—not an easy one. One student proudly brought in a real X-ray of her brother's foot. She held it up to the light to show us where his injury was. I suddenly realized that in the large round mass that she calling his foot, there were no bones visible. Odd ... it was, after all, a real X-ray. After closer examination, it was determined that although this was a real X-ray it wasn't of her brother's foot. It was her mother's mammography! I held myself back from telling her mother to send it back when we covered the letter M/m, but I really wanted to! That explained the no bones! (Note to parents— double-check what your child is bringing in for Show and Tell!)

What Happens in the Bathroom Should Stay in the Bathroom

Ah ... the bathroom. That's a whole other book! Many kindergartens have bathrooms right in their classrooms, which of course is very convenient yet very interesting. Five- and six-year-olds often forget to close the door while tending to their business or simply choose not to. Many boys feel it's perfectly appropriate to pull their pants up while walking across the class, and many a little girl has come out in her tights with skirt in hand. According to them, no one had ever explained that you don't have to take the whole thing off—you can simply pull down! The look of utter surprise when pointing out a more acceptable alternative to either gender is priceless. They think I'm a genius when I explain that it's better to pull your pants up *in* the bathroom—so innocent and so carefree!

We've also had quite a few rock stars enter our bathroom in kindergarten. It must be similar to adults in the shower who think they've missed their calling to be in a band—it's got to be the acoustics. I've heard fantastic renditions of everything from "God Bless America" to Bon Jovi's "Living on a Prayer" straight off the toilet seat. The best part is when they come out with a straight face as if they've just finished their first set. *American Idol,* kindergarten style.

Another interesting fact is that some children feel underwear is optional—I kid you not. I once had a little boy who came to school without underwear on a regular basis—he simply hated the tags on the back. Although his parents had given him underwear, he felt it put a crimp in his style. Parents, please double-check for proper undergarments. I'm not sure they are required by law, but they sure are appreciated.

Lunchtime

Some schools have snack time in the morning and lunchtime in the afternoon. Such is the case in a school where I was teaching. Lunchtime came and Kathleen told me her mom did not pack lunch—I found this odd. Her mother was very efficient; it would have been unlike her not to pack lunch, but hey, weirder things have happened. I went through Kathleen's lunch box, and sure enough it was empty. She said, "See, Mrs. Podest? I told you! She only packed me a snack." I then inquired about the snack. Kathleen replied, "I only had apple slices, a yogurt, cookies, a juice box, and a turkey and cheese sandwich." I think her mom had it covered. She just needed to show or label for her daughter what should be eaten and when.

You might also want to clarify with your child that if you send leftovers, they may not be as smoking hot as they are served at home. Many children bring in macaroni and cheese, pasta, soup, etc. in thermoses. One of my students named Lucy brought in empanadas one day. They looked and smelled delicious. Lucy was very excited about her lunch. She was all ready to eat when a perplexed look came upon her face. She scanned the room—something was amiss. "Mrs. Podest? Where's the heater upper? My empanadas aren't hot enough." The what? "The heater upper—you know, like you have in your kitchen." Well, poor Lucy had cold empanadas that day, but she was right; a heater upper (a.k.a. a microwave) sure would've been nice.

Some Other Favorite Misconceptions

One day when asking for the class to help me make a list of words that begin with the initial F/f sound, I got a few interesting answers. Enthusiastic hands went up and wide-eyed faces said, "Oh I know!" "Fun!" "Fat!" "Five!" "Fist!" "Ffffursday!"

"Ffffursday?" I asked.

"Yeah! You know—the day before Friday!"

One morning when the class was outside for morning recess, I noticed that the children were slowly lining up along the fence that faced a church. Soon enough the whole class was there and suddenly they broke out into applause. When I ran over to see what was going on, one of my favorite little Irishman named Sean said, "Listen, Mrs. Podest—a band!" It was actually a funeral procession, and they were playing the bagpipes for the deceased! I quickly called the children away and tried as hard as I could to contain my laughter. Only the eyes of a beautiful little five year old boy could see the joy in such sadness. I said a silent prayer for the soul of the deceased and at that moment thanked God for my career choice—I love what I do.

It was time to take our supplies as we were beginning a project. Everyone needed their scissors, crayons, and glue. Brendan raised his hand and sadly said, "I don't think I can do the project, I ran out of my Elvis." Your what? "My Elvis glue" (not to be confused with Elmer's!).

Kindergarten students love to ask how old you are and what your "real" name is. I always have fun with this and never tell them my age. I love the fact that they almost always have me a good twenty to thirty years younger than I really am. Occasionally I get really lucky and someone throws me into the late teenage years (straight As for that kid!). When it comes to my first name, many of them don't even realize I have one. One day two children came up to my desk and said, "Mrs. Podest, what is your real name?" (a.k.a. my first name). So I said with a very straight face, "Mrs." They looked at each other, made a face, and I heard one whisper to the other," That's *so* weird her parents named her that!"

The holiday season was rolling around, and everyone was in the spirit of giving. One of my little girls told me she and her brother wanted to do something for the poor, so they were giving all their old toys away—on eBay.

My own son was in kindergarten and brought an apple to school every day with his lunch. It was a Saturday in May, toward the very end of the year, and I was getting an apple out of the refrigerator for him.

When I handed it to him, he handed it back. I looked at him in confusion and he said, "Can you please slice it?"

I asked him when we started slicing apples instead of eating them whole.

He told me, "Well, Mrs. Gorman slices it for me every day."

I was mortified—I had no idea he had the aide in his class doing this for him! She must've thought, *What a lazy and presumptuous mother to think I'll do this every day.* But because of her sweet disposition, she didn't mind and did it every day with a smile.

Thank you, Mrs. Gorman.

Conclusion

This book has been a longtime collection of observations, notes, thoughts, experiences, ideas, obstacles, triumphs, and blessings along the road of my life as a mother and a teacher. As I stated earlier, I do not have all the answers when it comes to raising our children or sending them off to school. What I have to offer is my insight and what I have seen work and what I have seen prove fruitless. What have I learned along the way? I truly believe in my heart that most people in the world are doing the very best they can (myself included) at each particular moment in time. I have had so many moments in my own life that I wish I could erase or take back, things I've said or done.

But thank God I have so many more I am extremely proud of, that I took a chance or trusted my gut. There were moments where I took the time to really get to know a particularly challenging child or a difficult parent because I believed I was here for a reason to help. There have been teaching moments between children who were fighting where I could show them the good in each other—these moments helped shape my life as much as the theirs.

We all have different styles of parenting and teaching—respect each other's differences and try to learn from each other. Take a moment to step back and rethink a conversation that you had with someone or a situation you may have been in—did you handle that respectfully? Could you have done something different—or better?

Don't be afraid to confide in a friend when you are at the end of your parenting rope or don't know how to handle a situation in school. Other parents are the greatest resources in the world, and sharing experiences is the cheapest form of therapy there is. You always feel better when you know someone else has gone through what you may be going through and came out of it in one piece. Something I have learned is that I am a better mother and teacher for accepting the things I don't understand about other people or can't change and that all children are simply a product of their environment. There is absolutely *no* such thing as a bad child—children are simply what they learn.

What have I learned that I consider fruitless? Excessive worrying, comparing your children to someone else's children, getting upset with your children for not doing something they simply are not capable of yet, expecting from them more than they are able to deliver, and the worst offender of all time: not accepting your children for who they are, not who you always wanted them to be or who you think they should be.

Like every fingerprint in the world and every grain of sand on the beach, no two children are exactly alike, and I thank God for that every day. I embrace and cherish each child's uniqueness and feel I have been given a gift to see them all as complete, perfect individuals. Do the same for your children and you will be giving them the greatest gift in the world—true, unconditional love.

Oh—and while you're at it—do the same for yourself. Know that we, the parents and teachers, are all different as well, and we will all make mistakes. When you do mess up—and you will, I promise—forgive yourself. Then try to learn something from it. That's the greatest gift you can give yourself.

Thank you for taking the time to read this book and share my insights. In doing so, you have just shown yourself what a wonderful parent you truly are.

Acknowledgments

To my children Christian, Julia, Claire, and Aedan: I have treasured and loved watching you grow and become the people you are becoming—I could not be prouder. You are all so unique—so special in your own way. Don't ever change who you are.

To my husband, Brian, thank you for all your support and belief in me. You helped me find time to write when I thought I couldn't make time, you encouraged me when I thought I couldn't make this book happen, and you never stopped believing that I could really do this. I love you.

To my family and friends who have encouraged and supported me on this project, you reinforced for me that I wasn't totally crazy and that there was a real need and audience for this book—thank you. I especially want to thank my own parents—you were my very first teachers.

To the parents and teachers who have inspired me and reminded me how I felt in 2001 when my firstborn was starting kindergarten: there are so many wonderful and caring parents who are raising our future of tomorrow—keep doing what you are doing! Your children are blessed and so lucky to have you steering their course.

To my beautiful little angels—my students past and present—I am the luckiest person in the world. I marvel at your purity and innocence every day. Seeing the world through your eyes has been one of the greatest gifts of my life.

About the Author

Jeannie Podest is a wife, mother, and a teacher. She resides in suburban New Jersey with her husband of twenty years, their four children, and two dogs. She completed her undergraduate studies at Villanova University, earning her BA with a dual minor in psychology and sociology. She then earned her master's degree in elementary education at Pace University in White Plains, New York. She is certified to teach in both New Jersey and New York and has taught most grades from kindergarten through eighth grade. While she enjoys children of all ages, she has a special affinity for kindergarten, which she has taught in both private and public school. Jeannie has observed and learned so many valuable lessons along the way and sees herself as a perpetual student. She has compiled her lessons learned and shared them with you in this book so that you may begin your journey and your child's journey into kindergarten with ease and loving support.

In her spare time, Jeannie enjoys spending as much time outside as possible doing anything fun and active—running, bike riding, skiing, hiking—you name it! She is often found on a game field cheering on her children in their many different sports. She is a self-proclaimed "beach bum" and finds nothing more peaceful than a day with her toes in the sand, listening to the ocean waves crashing. She hopes that you will do the same sometime soon, with this book in your hands, as you prepare to embark on the next exciting stage of your child's life—kindergarten.

CPSIA information can be obtained at www.ICGtesting.com
Printed in the USA
BVOW03s0612160414

350740BV00001B/2/P